FEELING FREE

Supernatural Freedom from Anxiety, Depression, and Other Toxic Emotions

Terry Toler

Our books can be purchased in bulk for promotional, educational, and business use. Please contact your bookseller or the BeHoldings Publishing Sales department at sales@terrytoler.com.

For booking information email: booking@terrytoler.com

First U.S. Edition: January 2021
Printed in the United States of America
ISBN 978-1-7352243-9-8

About The Author

Terry Toler is a best selling and award winning author of seventeen books on success in the areas of marriage, health, and finance all centered around a relationship with Jesus Christ. He is also a prolific writer of fiction books including The Eden Stories along with several spy and mystery novels. Terry has been a motivational speaker and success counselor for more than thirty years and has helped thousands set goals for their life and then achieve them. Terry and his wife, Donna, live in Arkansas where they live out the principles of Feeling Free every day. He can be followed at terrytoler.com.

OTHER BOOKS BY TERRY TOLER

How to Make More Than a Million Dollars
The Heart Attacked
Seven Years of Promise
Mission Possible
Marriage Made in Heaven
21 Days to Physical Healing
21 Days to Spiritual Fitness
21 Days to Divine Health
21 Days to a Great Marriage
21 Days to Financial Freedom
21 Days to Sharing Your Faith
7 Days to Emotional Freedom
21 Days to Mission Possible
Suddenly Free
Uncommon Finances
Uncommon Health
Uncommon Marriage

Fiction Books

The Longest Day
The Reformation of Mars
The Great Wall of Ven-Us
Saturn: The Eden Experiment
The Late, Great Planet Jupiter
Save The Girls
The Ingenue
The Blue Rose

For more information on these books and other resources
visit TerryToler.com.

PLEASE READ BEFORE BEGINNING THIS BOOK

This is a faith-based book. The intention is not to offer or take the place of medical advice. Do not rely on it for the treatment or diagnosis of any medical or psychological condition. Please consult your health care provider for medical or mental health questions.

TABLE OF CONTENTS

PART ONE
WHY GOD GAVE YOU EMOTIONS

PART TWO
WHAT EMOTIONAL FREEDOM FEELS LIKE

PART ONE

WHY GOD GAVE YOU EMOTIONS

"Feelings can't be ignored, no matter how unjust or ungrateful they seem."
Anne Frank, *The Diary of a Young Girl*

1

A New Normal

"Are my feelings normal?"

A young woman asked me that question in a counseling session. She had been promiscuous as a teen, and when she became pregnant, the elders of the church made her stand in front of the congregation and confess her sin to everyone. The deep-seated shame of that traumatic experience still caused her deep emotional pain as an adult and was destroying her life and marriage.

When she asked, "Are my feelings normal?" I replied, "Yes. They are normal human emotions, but they are not what God intended for your life."

Negative emotions from traumatic circumstances are normal in the same sense that tornadoes in Oklahoma are normal, hurricanes on the gulf coast are normal, and earthquakes in California are normal. The word *normal* means usual or typical. It's usual or typical to struggle with negative emotions, especially when something bad happens, but that doesn't mean your negative emotions are any more acceptable than the behaviors or offenses that caused them.

We live in a fallen world. As the moral fabric of our society continues to erode, so does its emotional health. The number of people on mood-altering medications doubled from 1999 to 2012 according to a report in the *Journal of the American Medical Association.*

I could give you updated statistics, but is it really necessary?

We all intuitively know that emotional health in our society is eroding at an epidemic pace. Divorce, adultery, violent crime, sexual abuse, bankruptcy, sickness and disease, and other events that can cause emotional trauma, have increased exponentially over the last few years. As destructive behaviors increase, so do toxic emotions.

As if we needed any additional stress in our lives, a global pandemic has turned our world upside down. Is it any wonder we turn to medication, alcohol, drugs, promiscuity, and other addictive behaviors to mask the pain caused by the fallen world and an enemy intent on destroying us? Here is an important question to consider:

Wouldn't it make sense that if the behaviors are fallen, then our emotional response to the behaviors may be fallen as well?

My wife and I provide marriage counseling for our church. A couple came to us on the verge of divorce. He was struggling with intense anger and would explode with fits of rage at the slightest provocation. After talking for a few minutes, we learned that he was physically, sexually, and emotionally abused by his stepfather when he was a boy. His mother ignored the abuse and sided with her husband and kicked the boy out of the house at age thirteen.

He blamed himself for the abuse and suffered with feelings of abandonment. Later in his teens, he turned to drugs and alcohol so he could dull the pain. He had been clean and sober for two years but was about to lose his wife and family because of unresolved pain from seventeen years prior. His anger was not with his wife, even though that was where it was directed. His deep-seated anger was really toward his mom and stepdad and deep emotional hurts that were unresolved. Those past hurts were about to destroy his present reality.

At the same time, his wife was afraid of his outbursts and had developed great mistrust in his actions. She began to expect him to fall back into his addictions and resigned herself to the fact that he would never change. She had begun taking steps to withdraw from him emotionally to protect herself and her child from what she thought was an inevitable divorce.

His past hurts and her future worries were sabotaging their future. We asked them what their life would be like if the past hurts were resolved and there were no future worries. They acknowledged that their life would be great. They loved each other and believed God had brought them together for something great.

Then they both asked if their feelings were normal.

Is it normal for so many children to be sexually, physically, and emotionally abused? One in four girls and one in five boys will be sexually abused before the age of eighteen. It's becoming too "usual" and too "typical." What happened to him is becoming more and more widespread. The emotional fallout is normal as well. It's widely known that sexual abuse as a child creates depression, post-traumatic stress, behavioral problems, sexualized behavior, academic problems, a higher incidence of suicide, and it's common for victims to become the abusers. The feelings associated with abuse should not be considered normal, but unfortunately, they have come to be expected.

While what happened to this man as a child was destructive to his childhood, the toxic emotions from those childhood events are equally destructive to his adulthood. Here are some of the things we hear from people who have been devastated emotionally by the harmful actions of another person:

"I have a right to be angry."

"I will never trust anyone again."

"I will forgive, but I will never forget what he did to me."

"I am angry at God. Why would He let this happen to me?"

"I'm just not ready to forgive that person. He doesn't deserve my forgiveness."

"I want him to hurt as much as he has hurt me."

"I hate him. I hate her."

While all of those emotions are normal in the sense that we understand why someone would feel that way, they are still fallen emotions. They are not God's design and they only lead to toxicity that can lead to sickness, disease, and even death. More often than not, toxic emotions do more damage to a person than the original offense.

A high percentage of prostitutes have been sexually abused in the past. The emotional pain that comes from selling their bodies is generally far worse than the original sexual trauma they endured. They are responding to pain from their past with more destructive behaviors that cause even more psychological trauma.

Children of divorced parents are more likely to divorce their own spouses in the future. That is directly related to the emotional dysfunction of growing up in a home with only one parent or a stepparent.

Couples who divorce are more likely to divorce again if they remarry. Sixty-seven percent of second marriages and ninety percent of third marriages end in divorce. The emotional fallout from the first divorce carries over to the future marriages, making them less likely to be successful.

I call this, compounded troubles.

Suicides can often be traced back to past traumatic events. That is the ultimate example of the past hurt creating destructive behaviors in the present reality. Drug and alcohol dependency are often just an attempt to mask past pain. The problem is that the addiction makes things worse than they were.

It's well documented how destructive drugs and alcohol can be. They create many more problems than the ones they are trying to unsuccessfully mask. It's very typical for past traumas to create such toxic emotions that they produce more severe traumas in the present or future.

Not all negative emotions come from someone doing something harmful to you. Sometimes life just deals a tremendous blow.

Fallen Feelings

A woman lost a child. Her grief became so overwhelming she sunk into a deep depression. The pain was so debilitating she struggled to get out of bed in the morning and take care of her husband and three other children. When we talked to her about living in present reality, she came to realize she had to resolve the toxic emotions from the loss so that she didn't cause damage to those who were still living.

We've counseled couples on the verge of divorce because they couldn't handle the emotional fallout from a significant loss. The loss could be the death of a parent, child, sibling, or the loss of a business, church, job, or friendship. A perfectly good marriage can be destroyed from the emotional fallout of a traumatic situation not resolved when it happened. The divorce only makes things worse and creates more emotional pain that years later will be a past hurt.

When unexpected pain occurs in your life, it's "normal" to respond with negative feelings. Anyone would have sympathy for a mother who has lost her child. However, she has crossed over into what I call "fallen feelings." They are the emotional response to difficult circumstances based on the fall of man. They are not how God wants us to respond emotionally to troubles.

I was meeting with a man whose wife had had an affair a couple years before. She repented and ended the adulterous relationship and, after rebuilding trust with her husband, their marriage was restored. Even though a lot of time had passed, he was having a hard time getting over the feelings of betrayal. He said things like:

"Why would she do this to me?"

"When I think about her with him, it makes me so angry."

"When I picture them together, it just drives me crazy."

"What would she see in him? What is wrong with me? Is it because he is younger, better looking, more buff?"

The man joined a gym thinking he needed to make himself more attractive to his wife to compete against other men. Here were more of his thoughts:

"Maybe I should have an affair to get back at her."

"Sometimes I just look at her and wonder what she was thinking."

"Does she still think about him when she is with me?"

"I get these panic attacks and feel like I have to talk to her about it. She says that I make her feel guilty every time I bring it up."

"I can't seem to let it go. Why can't she understand that I put up with her having the affair, now I need time to express my feelings?"

"I don't know that I will ever be able to trust her again."

"How do I know that she is not going to do it again?"

"Am I normal to feel this way?"

I asked him, "What would your life be like today, if the only emotions you felt were based on what your life is like today, instead of being based on past hurts or future worries?"

He said, "My life would be great. We would be incredibly happy."

I asked him, "Is she having an affair today?"

"No," he replied.

"Then why are you angry with her today? She loves you. Focus on who she is in this moment and not on the sins of her past. Don't worry about what she might or might not do tomorrow. Love her today."

It's an unfortunate reality, but adultery has become a normal occurrence in many marriages. Approximately fifty percent of women and sixty percent of men will have an extramarital affair. The emotions of betrayal are deep and devastating. The emotions are inevitable which is why God said not to do it. It's normal to have those emotions in times of crisis, but it's still not what God originally intended. God never intended for a married man or woman to become one flesh with someone other than their spouse, and God never intended for jealousy, anger, and unforgiveness to last indefinitely.

Galatians 5:19 says that the lust of the flesh are sexual immorality, impurity, and orgies among other things. Everyone can agree that those are horrible sins and devastating to relationships. We can also agree that those are normal behaviors in the sense that they have become too commonplace and too typical in our society.

Do you know what else made the list? Anger, jealousy, dissensions, selfishness, and strife. They are listed right after witchcraft and idolatry.

The common, usual, and typical emotions for the betrayed spouse are anger, jealousy, selfishness, and strife. The betrayed man we discussed fell prey to all of those sinful feelings. They were consuming him to the point that he was sabotaging the restoration God was doing in their marriage. That is typical behavior. The Bible categorizes his toxic emotions in the same list as adultery.

Fallen behavior is most often met with fallen emotions. Both are equally devastating. We have given our toxic emotions way too much power by allowing them to become so acceptable in our lives. Our response of eye for an eye is killing millions of people from the inside out. It is prolonging suffering and disease.

Recently, while attending a Christian conference on emotional healing, one of the certified therapists continually told the audience, "You need to honor your pain. Honor your grief. Own your feelings. Validate your brokenness." As well-meaning as those thoughts are, and at first take, they seem logical, but after hearing it over and over, it became clear that many psychologists and therapists are trying to solve deep spiritual issues with strategies and tactics that are simply not Biblical.

Why are we to honor feelings that are classified as lust of the flesh? Where, in Scripture, does God say to give honor to grief or other prolonged toxic emotions?

According to the verse in Galatians, jealousy, strife, anger, and dissensions towards an unfaithful spouse, while understandable, are as toxic as the lust of the flesh and sexual immorality. Imagine attending a Christian conference where the speaker said, "You need to honor your feelings of lust. Acknowledge and own your feelings of adultery or fornication. Embrace your feelings of anger. Validate your love for pornography."

Doesn't that sound crazy to you? It does to me. But that is what happens when we give power to emotions and validate them. We are teaching people that anger is acceptable. Greed is tolerated. Strife is normal, and negative emotions should be expected when someone makes a mistake. The Bible, however, says that anger is supposed to be resolved the "same day" you feel angry about something.

"Don't let your anger go down with the sun" the Scripture admonishes us.

Many people, like the man whose wife committed adultery, hold on to anger for years, even decades. Anger is the fallen emotion that compounds the troubles from the original sin of the woman's affair. Both are missing the mark of God's best.

Feelings Give us Information

God gave us positive emotions to enjoy life. He gave us negative emotions to give us information. For instance, God gave us fear so we could identify a dangerous situation. If you are walking in the woods and see a bear, you will feel fear and you will know that you need to get out of the dangerous situation.

Many people struggle with fear when there is no danger. That is because the emotion is used in a way that God never intended. The Bible says 365 times to "fear not." It says that God has not given us a spirit of fear. Why would we ever want to own feelings of fear? Why would we ever want to validate them or honor them?

The Bible says to be anxious for nothing. Why would we honor anxiety or allow it to be acceptable? God never intended for feelings to be anything more than short-term and our body's way of giving us useful information.

Perhaps you have suffered for years from anxiety, fear, eating disorders, suicidal thoughts, pornography, anger, various addictions, bitterness, resentment, sadness, unforgiveness, abuse, shame, and/or deep depression and loneliness. Maybe you have experienced a very painful past or made decisions you deeply regret. Perhaps you have been abused physically, verbally, or sexually. Maybe you have had severe traumas, and life has been hard and seemingly unfair. Maybe you have suffered the devastating loss of a loved one and are consumed with ongoing grief. It's possible, maybe even probable, that your feelings have become normal to you. Perhaps they have even become a coping mechanism that you rely on for comfort.

When horrible things happen to us, there are typical and usual feelings that result. That is normal. What is not normal is for the feelings to gain control over you and become a part of the fabric of your emotional DNA. That is what this book is about. I want to help you create a new normal. I want to help you experience the freedom of a life without toxic emotions. That will happen when you realize why God gave you emotions.

Emotions are for Present Reality

God gave us emotions to be short-term and based on present reality. Instead, we have made emotions like anchors based on past hurts, future worries, and compounded with present troubles. That is when emotions become overwhelming. God never intended for you to deal today with emotions from your past or emotions related to something that might or might not happen in the future. He gave us enough grace for today's troubles but not enough for compounded emotions.

This is why forgiveness, faith, trust, and focusing on good things is so commonly encouraged throughout Scripture. God created you to feel and deal with toxic emotions on a day-to-day basis without anchoring them in your soul for extended periods of time.

The etymology of the word "emotion" gives us some insight as to what it actually means. Motion, of course, means movement. "E" means out or exit. The word "emotion" literally means to move out. That is what God intended when He gave you feelings. Emotions are meant to be felt and then moved out of your life as quickly as possible. Depression, anxiety, bitterness, resentment, unforgiveness, fear, discontent, etc. are all emotions that are held inside and when not released, take root in your life. That is not what God intended for you.

Back to the illustration of the bear in the forest. Fear is a God-given gift that lets you know your life is in danger and you need to flee. If, however, you allow fear to linger, even when there are no bears around, you now become prey to a "spirit" of fear. This is not God's design.

If you hear a noise in your house during the middle of the night, it's okay for your fight or flight emotions to be triggered, causing you to investigate whether an intruder has entered your home. If you remain in fear for days or weeks to come once you realize there was never any danger, fear has entered your heart and a toxic emotion has taken root.

In a similar way, anger is supposed to be short-term. Anger gives you the information that someone has offended you or there has been some kind of injustice. It may tell you that you need to remove yourself from having anything to do with that person. Anger may tell you that you need to confront him or her in order to bring relational healing or restoration. It may tell you that you need to forgive and walk away. Whatever information it gives you can be helpful in the short-term.

When the anger surfaces, you thank it for the information and then tell it to go away until the next time it's needed. You don't need the anger to confront the person. Anger is merely an emotional tool that gives you momentary courage to set wrong things in order.

The Bible says to be angry but not to sin. You sin when you direct your anger outward toward another human being. Instead of using it as information, you are using anger to hurt someone else who has hurt you. If you don't resolve your anger quickly, then you can feel the toxic emotions of unforgiveness indefinitely.

God never intended for you to feel anger for weeks, months, or years. You are not to let the sun go down on your anger, meaning that it's not supposed to last for more than one day. Long-term anger turns into bitterness; bitterness turns into anxiety and depression. Anger, when prolonged, can create long term health problems that lead to high blood pressure, stress, and even death.

Toxic Emotions Can Cause Pain for Years

A woman on *Good Morning America* related that she had been gang raped in college. She doesn't remember the actual rape because she was drugged the night it happened. Even though it was more than twenty years before, she was still living with devastating emotions. She lives with the fear of being alone with another man. She is afraid to walk down the street day or night by herself.

She can't experience sexual intimacy with her husband and has nightmares. Even though she doesn't remember the rape, she created her own images and replays the movie over and over in her mind. She's on medication, but it's merely masking the pain. After years of counseling and therapy, she still hasn't uprooted the spirit of fear that has taken root in her life. The rape was bad enough, but the emotional bondage due to fear has been so much worse. She has felt the emotions of the rape every day for twenty years.

What if she only felt emotions based on her present reality? What if she could be set free from all of the past hurts? What if she could be free from the worries of what might happen to her in the future? Her life was rather good in the present reality. Her past, however, was ruining her mental and emotional health. If she could focus on her present reality, she could have a wonderful life with her husband.

Instead, she is being tormented from something that's not happening in the present. God only intends for you to feel emotions that are happening now. Paul said to forget the past and Jesus said to not worry about the future. It's clear God wants you to only focus on your current troubles, immediate emotions, and on what is happening in the present moment. For that to happen to the woman who was raped, she would have to have her mind renewed and allow God to heal her emotions. She needs to be set free.

All at Once

Today is the first day of the rest of your life. That being the case, how would you like to live the rest of your life free from the pain of toxic emotions and addictions? It can happen. In fact, I believe it will happen for you. The Bible is filled with examples of people who were instantly changed by an encounter with God.

You may have given up hope a long time ago that things would change. Perhaps you have settled into a life of accepting your emotional pain and have learned to deal with it and have allowed it to become part of your new normal. What would it mean to you, your family, and your future if you could be free from every emotion, addiction, heartache, and sickness that has caused you pain?

What if it could happen all at once?

It can! In this book, I'm going to share with you real stories, from real people who have been transformed and "feel free" by focusing on present reality. Freedom doesn't mean all your problems will suddenly disappear or that life will no longer have times of troubles or testing. It does, however, mean you will be set free from the pain and bondage that have caused you to stay enslaved by your emotions.

One story in the Bible is about a prophet named Elijah. It says Elijah was a man with emotions like ours. He learned one day that a wicked woman, named Jezebel, who was the wife of a king, had vowed to kill him. Despite being a powerful man of God, he was so emotionally distraught by her threats, he fled to the desert in fear of his life. He finally grew so tired of running he laid down next to a bush and said, "I have had enough, Lord. Take my life." He laid down in his depression and fell asleep from the exhaustion.

His emotional pain and fear were so intense that he was on the verge of suicide. His fear, anxiety, and loneliness were so overwhelming he had given up on life and wanted to die. Have you ever felt that way? Have you ever said to God, "I've had enough, I can't take it anymore, and I want to die?" Have you ever wanted to lay down and fall asleep just to get some relief from the pain of this world?

Maybe things have never been that bad for you, but everyone has felt overwhelming emotions at one time or another. We've all been in a place where we needed God to help us with our emotional pain.

While Elijah was asleep, something miraculous happened. An angel of the Lord appeared "all at once" and touched him. Food and water miraculously appeared, and the angel told him to eat, drink and be strengthened. He got up and went on his journey and Jezebel was never able to kill him because the Lord protected him.

It happened for Elijah "all at once." Suddenly! What a powerful moment of transformation. For a brief moment, Elijah lost all hope. But that's when God's presence suddenly showed up and took control. Do you believe that kind of sudden freedom and empowerment can happen to you today? No matter what you are going through, no matter how difficult things may seem, no matter how depressed, anxious, or fearful you might feel in this moment, that same process of sudden transformation can happen to you.

It doesn't have to take weeks, months, or years. You don't have to beg God for freedom or live with emotional pain as a long-term diagnosis. You don't have to go through years of therapy or expense thousands of dollars on relief. Instead, it can happen suddenly. In fact, it has already happened.

You have an advantage over Elijah that you will grow to learn more about in this book. Elijah needed a rescuing angel to deliver him from his adversary and emotional brokenness. Today, you and

I have the Holy Spirit living inside of us. He is our Comforter, Counselor, and Guide sent by God to help us navigate our emotions and rescue us from all tactics of the enemy.

Feeling free defies logic. It is a supernatural gift of the Holy Spirit. If you approach freedom from an intellectual, psychological, or human perspective, you will need to take this course or another freedom course several times until you "get it." This is why many people go through years of recovery classes, therapy sessions, or freedom courses. But it doesn't have to be that way. When Jesus suddenly does what He is about to do in your life, you will never be the same. You will be suddenly free and new life will begin.

Are you ready? Let's get started on your pathway to freedom.

2
The Genesis of Emotions

"I hate the sound of my own voice."

"If I sang happy birthday at a birthday party, I would sound lousy."

Those words were spoken by Barbra Streisand. Streisand holds the Billboard chart record for the most number-one albums by a female artist. She has sold 150 million records, has nine Golden Globes, and is one of the few EGOTs—entertainers who have won an Emmy, Grammy, Oscar, and Tony Award. Her self-doubt stems from an event in June 1967. Streisand was performing live in front of 150,000 people in Central Park. She explained in her own words what happened:

> "I actually forgot the words. I was having some other kind of problems, and stage fright had set in, and in the middle of one of my songs, I just absolutely went blank. I still have that fear today, so I never performed for twenty-seven years unless it was for a political event or something."

Streisand was so emotionally traumatized by that one incident that she refused to perform live for twenty-seven years. The invention of teleprompters convinced her that she could perform again. In 1986, she was singing "America the Beautiful" with teleprompters at a *One Voice Concert*. When she started the song, the audience stood out of respect. The problem was that the teleprompters were on the ground, and when the audience stood, they blocked her view of the words. Even though she knew the words, she froze. The television producers had to use footage from her dress rehearsal for the broadcast. Streisand said in an interview about that event:

"It was such a traumatic moment in front of so many people and I still have that fear today that it could happen again."

According to reports, the only way she can perform live today is with a teleprompter properly positioned and by taking a pill called Inderal, which is a beta-blocker that slows the heart and calms panic attacks. Other emotional traumas in her life have affected her ability to sing in public as well.

She once said, "When I felt guilty about leaving my first husband, I lost my voice. All of a sudden, I found myself on stage and couldn't hold a note, and I started thinking about how I do this."

Emotional trauma from the past has so much potential power that it can debilitate even the most talented individuals in the present.

The Past is Not the Present

"I'm not afraid of flying; I just fear I'm going to die. I think I'm
—vulnerable. I admit it. I don't fly. I got claustrophobia. I don't
go in high buildings. I don't do those things. I'm just myself,
whatever that is."
—John Madden

John Madden was an NFL coach and famous television commentator for many years. He was known as a hard-nosed, tough player, and coach. Obviously, it takes a lot of courage to play football and be on television. He was not afraid to take a hard hit, lose a big game, or risk making a mistake on live television.

However, Madden was afraid to fly and suffered from panic attacks when he flew. Eventually, Madden quit flying, purchased an RV, and used it to travel to games. For years, he would rarely get on a plane and only when he had no other choice. Why did he have so few fears in other areas of his life but had such a debilitating fear in that one area?

On October 29, 1960, a plane carrying members of the Cal Poly San Luis Obispo football team crashed, killing twenty-two of forty-eight passengers. John Madden was the graduate assistant for the team and was supposed to be on the flight but stayed behind to coach a junior varsity game. After that event, Madden began to have panic attacks on flights. In 1979, he had a major panic attack on a flight originating in Tampa. After that experience, he quit coaching so he wouldn't have to fly again.

Was the fear really of dying? The National Highway Safety Transportation Administration compiled statistics comparing flying and driving. The odds of dying in a plane crash are one in eleven million. The odds of dying in a car crash are about one in one hundred. Flying is much safer than driving. The fear was not based on anything logical. It was based on a past traumatic situation invading his present reality and creating a future worry that he might die in a plane crash. It is called aerophobia.

Madden drove hundreds of thousands of miles in a vehicle to avoid flying because he was afraid of dying. Ironically, driving statistically increased his percentage of dying. Vehophobia is a fear of driving in a car. Many people who have traumatic car crashes are afraid to drive or ride in a moving vehicle. It's the same fear that Madden has, only it's related to cars and not planes.

Madden's was related to a plane because that was the connection to his fear. He had no problem driving in an RV because he had no connection to a fear of driving in a vehicle. A person with vehophobia may not have a fear of flying. Their fear is connected to a traumatic car accident. Both are based on a connection to a past traumatic event and aren't related to anything happening in present reality.

Madden said in one quote that claustrophobia also contributes to his fear of flying. Many people suffer from claustrophobia while riding in an RV. What seems easier for one person is a bigger struggle for another. Madden feels claustrophobic in a plane but not an RV. Some people feel claustrophobic in an RV but not a plane. The fear is not with the activity but with the emotional connection to a trauma.

John didn't suffer the same stage fright from which Streisand suffered. In 1979, John Madden coached the Oakland Raiders to a win in the Super Bowl. That is the biggest stage in the world of football. Madden was also the commentator for eight Super Bowls—a live event with an estimated one-hundred-million viewers. That didn't faze Madden at all. He had no fear of speaking on live television in front of a hundred-million people. Streisand is petrified to sing in front of people. To my knowledge, she has no fear of flying.

It's important to understand that the activity is not the problem; it's the connection to a trauma in the past that produces the negative emotion.

Break the Connection

The world operates on connections. You plug a lamp into the wall and the light comes on. You hook a water line to the main and water flows to the house. Someone dials a cell phone and, when it's answered, a connection is made. We make emotional connections to events all the time. When something traumatic happens in our lives, a negative emotional response can become associated with that event. When we participate in that activity in the present, the emotions felt at the time of the past trauma connect with our present reality. We then feel the same emotions that we felt when the original traumatic event happened.

Every time Streisand gets up to sing, her emotions connect her present reality with her past trauma. She then experiences the same emotions she felt at the time of the trauma in her present reality even though the same trauma is not occurring. Every time Madden gets on a plane, he's afraid he's going to die, because his friends died more than sixty years ago. When he thinks about flying in a plane, he feels the emotions he felt from the original trauma when he suffered that devastating loss and the fear he felt since he was supposed to be on the plane.

This can happen with any trauma. A person who was raped may feel the same fear she felt at the time of the rape even though she's not in the same circumstance and is in no danger of being raped. A person who suffered the trauma of an intruder in his house, may feel the same fear every time he hears a noise in the house. A person who survives a bear attack, may be afraid to walk in the woods even if there is no bear within miles of him.

Part of the process of overcoming the emotions is understanding that they are not relevant in present reality but are rooted in a connection to the past. You overcome them by breaking the connection. It's also important to understand that the connection is not actually to the trauma; the connection goes back to the beginning of time.

Break the Connection to the Fall

Even God feels emotions. Throughout the Bible, God expressed many positive emotions. Nehemiah 8 talks about the joy of the Lord; Psalm 103:8 talks about God's compassion; John 3:16 talks about

God's love. When God expresses emotions, He is always true to His character and personality. His emotions are always expressed perfectly and exactly how emotions were intended to be expressed. That was also His original plan when He gave man emotions.

When God created man, He created him in His image with the same emotional characteristics. God created us with the capacity to feel every emotion that He feels. You were wonderfully and creatively made (Psalms 139:14), so your emotions were a wonderful part of God's design. God gave you feelings, cravings, likes, and dislikes for a purpose.

In the Garden of Eden, Adam and Eve's emotions were perfect, and all they felt were positive emotions. Feelings were expressed exactly as God had designed them. God expressed emotion after He finished with creation. He said it was very good! Exclamation point! God was pleased with His creation. That sounds like a positive emotional response to a job well done. When God created Adam and Eve, He was especially pleased with His handiwork and expressed His happiness with creating man.

Adam and Eve felt the same way. They lived with good and healthy emotions based on positive things that were happening. Admittedly, it was easier then, than it is now in that they had no troubles. They were happy because God was happy.

For a period of time, Adam and Eve had no reason to feel any negative emotions. Not much is said about the day-to-day interactions with each other, but you can imagine with some certainty that their lives were free from conflict, pain, anger, depression, sadness, or any other negative emotion.

The Bible says that they "felt" no shame in the garden. That tells us that they had the capacity to feel. Adam and Eve had feelings, but they didn't have negative feelings like shame. They were capable of feeling shame, but those feelings didn't manifest because they hadn't yet sinned and had no reason to feel shame. Their focus was on God and His creation and perfect interaction with each other.

Instead of feeling shame, they were walking in perfection. Remember, Adam named every animal on the earth. What an amazing feeling he must've felt through the core of his being. Both Adam and Eve had been given authority over everything on the earth and God blessed them. They were in perfect unity with each other. They must have felt an immense sense of satisfaction as they ruled the earth with their God-given authority. They, like God, probably looked at their work and said that it was very good.

Can you imagine the tremendous joy and peace they felt when they communed with God in the cool of the evening? They certainly "felt" pleasure when they were with each other. Becoming one flesh with Eve must have certainly brought feelings of love and contentment to both of them.

Unfortunately, in a single moment, with a single choice, everything changed, and their positive emotions became negative in one moment of sin. The crafty and deceptive serpent appeared and played on their human emotions and tricked them into believing his lies. He challenged their belief in God. He said they would "become like God" if they ate of the fruit. Greed and rebellion were put in front of them as temptation. Perfect human emotions were manipulated and twisted into selfish ambition for the first time.

When Adam and Eve consumed the forbidden fruit, they unknowingly chose to separate themselves from God and gave their authority over the earth to Satan. In that single moment, sin entered the world, and pain, sorrow, depression, shame, hate, bitterness, fear, and an onslaught of other dark emotions entered the world as well. In one moment of choice, Adam and Eve relinquished the power God had given to them and surrendered their emotions to the enemy.

After he ate the fruit, Adam told God that he was hiding because he was afraid. That was a new emotion for Adam. He had never been afraid of God before that day. Before sin, Adam only had the knowledge of good emotions. Suddenly, he had the knowledge of evil and bad emotions and the feelings that came with them.

Adam and Eve hid because they were ashamed for the first time. Before sin, they lived in the garden naked and unashamed. Once sin entered the world, so did the negative emotion of shame.

Had man never sinned, we would still be living with perfect emotions in the garden. You would always be capable of negative emotions, but they would never have manifested in your everyday life. Today, you live with the knowledge of good and evil and the ability to experience negative emotions. Those negative emotions are a result of Adam and Eve's sin. Sin and death and negative emotions have spread from Adam and Eve to your life.

Jesus Broke the Connection to the Fall

Darlene Zschech started performing at age ten on an Australian children's show called *Happy Go Round*. At age thirteen, her parents divorced. The emotional stress of her parent's break up was so traumatic that she struggled with bulimia for four years. She came to know Christ at fifteen, and her life began to change, but she still struggled with self-doubt. She had so many insecurities she quit performing for several years.

In 1993, she wrote a worship song called *Shout to the Lord*. She related that she wrote it during a time of deep personal struggle. Even if you are saved you can still deal with emotional pain from the past. She worked at Hillsong Church in Australia as a secretary. One day she told the worship leader of the church that she had written a new song, and he said that he wanted to hear it. She was so embarrassed to play it for him that she made him stand with his back to her while she played and sang him the song. He loved the song, and the rest is history. *Shout to the Lord* is the most sung modern worship song in history.

In addition, Darlene has sung live to millions of people across the world in some of the largest venues in the world. How did she go from being so emotionally insecure that she would not sing facing one person, to singing to tens of thousands in one setting? She credits the Holy Spirit for breaking the emotional connection between her fear of performing and creating a different connection to her calling to lead others in worship.

> "I grappled with the whole performance issue when I first got saved when I was 15. I stopped singing for a few years because I couldn't stop doing what I was trained to do. Then one day the Holy Spirit just nailed me and said, 'you don't need to perform for Me.' That thing rears its ugly head every now and again and it has to be put to death. But that's life in Christ, learning how to die so you can live."

When she performed, she was afraid of failure and what people might think of her. When she understood that she was worshiping God, that He wasn't concerned about her performance, that she couldn't fail in His eyes, then the emotional connection to the fear of failure was broken. The insecurities were replaced with faith in God.

You will always have the capacity to feel negative emotions because you are made in the image of God, and you were born with the knowledge of good and evil and a connection to the fall. However, Christ came to restore God's original intent for man in the garden. So, while you have the capacity to feel the negative emotions of fear, anxiety, depression, guilt, shame, condemnation, anger, bitterness, and resentment, Christ has made a provision for you to choose to let

Him restore your emotions to their original intent. That should give you hope. Christ broke the connection to negative emotions.

Darlene can sing on stage in front of thousands without the aid of medication or the fear of failure because Christ has destroyed the connection between her present reality and what happened in the garden when sin entered the world. He also broke the emotional connections to her parent's divorce and her bulimia. She still has the capacity to feel the insecurity and negative emotions, she just has a new connection with the Holy Spirit and Christ who strengthens her to be able to do all things.

This book is about breaking the emotional connection to your past hurts and your future worries and focusing on your present reality. Even though you may know Jesus broke the emotional connection to the fall, that doesn't mean you don't still feel those negative emotions. Keep reading, and you'll see how Jesus also gave you the power to break the connection to the emotions once and for all.

3

Negative Emotions Are Meant to be Short-Term

When sin entered the world, so did negative emotions. As we have seen, man and God lived in perfect harmony before the fall. No one displayed negative emotions and the world was void of emotional pain and suffering. After the fall, man not only had to deal with his own negative emotions, but he had to live with God expressing what would be considered negative emotions. Here are a few of them:

Anger: Numbers 32:13 says God's anger burned against Israel.

Regret: Genesis 6:6 says that God regretted making man and His heart was deeply troubled.

Jealousy: Exodus 20:5 says that God was jealous when the children of Israel started worshiping other gods.

Grief: Psalm 78:40 says that God was grieved by the actions of His people in the wasteland.

Hatred: Malachi 2:16 says that God hates divorce. Proverbs 6:16 says there are six things God hates and seven that are detestable to Him.

Since God created man with the ability to experience negative emotions and knowing that man would eventually fall and experience them, God must have had a purpose for creating man with those emotions. Negative emotions can be useful when applied as God originally intended. When emotions are not used in the way

God intended, then they become sin. They miss the mark of their original purpose.

So, how does God want you to live with negative emotions and yet do so without sinning? Since God is perfect and you are made in His image, you can learn how to deal with emotions by understanding the nature and characteristics of God and how He handles emotions. Let's look at how God handles two specific emotions: anger and sorrow.

God's Anger Only Lasts for a Moment

For his anger lasts only a moment, but his favor lasts a lifetime.

♡ (Psalms 30:5) ♡

Anger is a powerful emotion given to us by God. However, God modeled for us that anger is only supposed to last for a short period of time. Things are going to happen in this fallen world to make you angry just like Adam and Eve made God angry when they ate from the tree. Adam and Eve totally thwarted God's plan for their life. God was so angry with them that He cursed them and threw them out of the garden and placed armed guards at the gate. However, before God threw them out of the garden, He made them clothes.

Remember that they were naked and ashamed. Even in His anger, God was still protecting them and showing them love and concern for their well-being. Also note that God never mentioned Adam and Eve's sin again. God was angry, dealt with it, got over it, never brought it up again, and restored favor to Adam and Eve almost immediately and blessed them with children.

God wants to do the same thing for you and wants you to do the same thing for others. Something will inevitably make you angry. When anger comes, resolve it immediately so it doesn't become a toxic emotion.

> "Be angry, and do not sin": do not let the sun go down on
> your wrath.
> (Ephesians 4:26 NKJV)

Anger is not supposed to last longer than a day. The Bible also says that when you are angry, you're not supposed to sin. Anger can be a positive emotion when you're angry at an injustice or a wrong. Anger can motivate you to help fix the injustice. Anger can turn to sin when directed toward the person instead of the injustice itself. Anger becomes hurtful to you when it lasts for longer than a moment.

A couple who had a huge fight the week before came in for counseling. It started with something minor, but it escalated into a hurtful scene. As we explored why they were fighting, it became obvious they were still angry over something that had happened two years before. Their anger had been building like a pressure cooker.

She was depressed, and he had become mean and emotionally abusive. The unresolved anger was building like a volcano ready to explode. That's why God says to deal with anger immediately. Anger escalates each time you become angry without resolving it. Eventually, almost anything can set you off.

Jesus Felt Anger

> Jesus entered the Temple and began to drive out all the people
> buying and selling animals for sacrifice. He knocked over the tables
> of the money changers and the chairs of those selling doves.
> (Matthew 21:12)

In Jesus's day, a worshiper had to come to the Temple with an animal sacrifice. If they didn't have one, they could buy one. The problem was that the local merchants only accepted local coins. Greedy businessmen set up locations inside of the Temple to sell animals and exchange money. They were charging exorbitant rates and taking advantage of the people. They would have been providing a good service to the people if they had been fair in their dealings with them. Jesus was indignant because they were not only taking advantage of the people, but they were doing so in a house of worship. He said they had turned His temple into a den of thieves.

This is what God intended when He gave us anger. Anger is an emotion given to us by God to respond to an injustice. It wasn't designed to be used against those who offend us. If someone has offended us, Matthew 18 says to go to a brother privately and discuss it with him. If that doesn't work, take another person and ultimately bring it before the church.

If anyone is angry over the offense, they aren't to sin in that anger. Galatians 6:1 says that if a brother sins, that we are to restore him gently. It's God's kindness that leads to repentance, not anger. We sin when we hold the anger in longer than a moment or use it to hurt someone who has hurt us. We sin when we lash out at another person in anger. The Bible says that they will know we are Christians by our love.

Jesus modeled for us how anger is supposed to be used against an injustice. Anger has to serve a higher purpose. This wasn't Jesus's first trip to Jerusalem. Jesus had seen the moneychangers in the Temple before that day. His anger was withheld at those times until His anger could be used for a greater purpose. Driving out the moneychangers was the final straw that ultimately caused the religious leaders to have Jesus arrested. Part of God's plan was to engineer circumstances so Christ would go to the cross.

Have you ever thought about using your anger strategically based on God's plans rather than your own selfish desire to hurt someone because they hurt you?

31

Do you know what Jesus did right after He overturned the moneychangers? Even though Jesus was angry, what happened next was amazing. Jesus's anger only lasted for a moment. A short time later, He was compassionately healing the blind and the lame. Jesus had complete control over His anger. He could feel anger in the moment, but then the anger was gone when it was no longer needed.

Right after that, the children gathered around Jesus and shouted His praises. One minute, Jesus was driving out the thieves with a whip; the next moment He was ministering to the sick and worshiping with children.

That isn't how most people handle their anger. Many hold on to their anger for days. They talk to everybody they know about how angry they are about something someone did to them. It can even affect their relationships and work. Some people get so angry they can't sleep at night. Many respond by being withdrawn or aloof. Others respond by lashing out and wearing their emotions on their sleeves. Others are passive aggressive and want the person to know they are angry but won't actually confront the situation and resolve it.

We had a woman in counseling who was so angry at her husband for an affair he'd had a couple of years before that she would not let it go. We finally suggested that she compose a letter to him and write down everything she was feeling. We encouraged her to not hold anything back and put all of her anger down on paper. Then we told her to tear up the letter. She insisted that she wanted to show it to him first. She wanted him to know all the ways in which he had hurt her. We explained that wanting to hurt him with her anger was sin.

She got angry at us!

She said, "He is the one who committed adultery and you're telling me I'm the one who is sinning!"

She didn't like the fact that God had forgiven him and resented that God was trying to restore him and that he had repented and asked for forgiveness. She didn't think he should be able to get off that easily. Our response to sin and offense is often anger. God's response in the new covenant is just the opposite:

> Don't you see how wonderfully kind, tolerant, and patient God is with you? Does this mean nothing to you? Can't you see that his kindness is intended to turn you from your sin? (Romans 2:4)

The above verse is clear about how God deals with us in our sin in the new covenant of grace. When we sin, it is not God's anger that brings us to repentance. In the Old Testament, God used His anger to punish in a moment. In the new covenant of grace, his kindness, tolerance, and patience brings us to repentance.

> If another believer is overcome by some sin, you who are godly should gently and humbly help that person back onto the right path. (Galatians 6:1)

If someone sins and commits an offense against us or against others, our response is not supposed to be anger. Our response should be to try gently and humbly to help that person get back on the right track. That is true even in the situation of adultery. Our first concern should be for the restoration of the spouse back to a right relationship with God. We should work with God's kindness to restore him or her. Then we should try to restore the marriage if possible.

Anger hinders restoration. It's meant to punish and hurt the offending person. God wants to restore him with kindness. In the case of adultery, that doesn't mean that the betrayed spouse has to stay with the person. Jesus said that spouses are free to divorce their husband or wife if they commit adultery. But Jesus didn't say that there has to be a long, drawn-out, divorce battle full of anger, bitterness, and animosity.

And if an offended spouse decides that he or she is going to stay in the marriage and make it work, then they should resolve their anger immediately with forgiveness and soften their hearts so that God can bring restoration through kindness and mercy rather than through anger and revenge.

> One day some parents brought their children to Jesus so he could touch and bless them. But the disciples scolded the parents for bothering him. When Jesus saw what was happening, he was **angry** with his disciples. He said to them, "Let the children come to me. Don't stop them! For the Kingdom of God belongs to those who are like these children. I tell you the truth, anyone who doesn't receive the Kingdom of God like a child will never enter it." Then he took the children in his arms and placed his hands on their heads and blessed them. (Mark 10:13-16 Emphasis added)

Jesus was angry at His disciples but used the opportunity as a teaching moment. He didn't judge them or make them feel bad about themselves. He corrected them and then took the children in His arms and blessed them. He was angry, but only for a moment. The anger quickly went away, and Jesus returned to His normal and loving demeanor. He didn't hold a grudge and act distant or aloof to His disciples because they had wrongly tried to turn away the children. He was angry, responded in anger without hurting the disciples, resolved it, and went back to expressing emotions appropriate for the moment.

Have you ever lashed out at your children in anger because you were mad at your spouse or someone at work? Jesus modeled not to do that. He did not let His anger affect His relationship with others.

Some people openly express their anger in front of their children. That can have devastating effects on their emotional health. So many couples who come to us for counseling, relate behavioral problems in their children. Even though Jesus was angry at the disciples, He controlled himself so that the children didn't even notice. He still kept such a loving demeanor, even though He was angry, the children were His first priority.

Can your anger be so short-term and so controlled that no one around you even knows you are angry? Even then, if you read the rest of the account, Jesus doesn't bring up the situation to His disciples again. He dealt with it, said what He needed to say to them, and then moved on and never brought it up again. The same thing is true of sorrows.

Sorrows Should have a 24-Hour Expiration Date

So the Lord was sorry he had ever made them and put them on the
earth. It broke his heart.
(Genesis 6:6)

After the fall, man became so sinful that God was sorry that He ever made man. The Bible says His heart was broken. Another translation says, "He was deeply troubled." God feels the same range of emotions that we feel only He does so without sinning. In this life, things are going to happen that create sorrows and pain. However, God models for us that the pain is supposed to be temporary and resolved almost immediately.

Weeping may last through the night, but joy comes
with the morning.
(Psalm 30:5)

35

According to this passage, we may experience sorrow, but like anger, it should not last longer than a day. By the next morning, it should be replaced with joy. When sorrow is allowed to last beyond a day, it can turn into depression. The symptoms of depression are:

1. Decreased energy or fatigue.
2. Sleeplessness.
3. Loss of interest in activities. Loss of motivation and desire.
4. Fixation on the past.
5. Worries about the future.
6. Thoughts of death or suicide. Feelings of hopelessness.
7. Extreme irritability.

Those things don't happen overnight. It takes prolonged periods of sadness to have that type of an effect on behavior. Depression, by definition, is long-term. An economic depression is an extended period of economic decline. An emotional depression is an extended period of sadness and sorrow. While all sorrow does not turn into depression, sorrow that's not resolved quickly does always lead to some physical manifestation including loss of appetite or overeating, weight gain or loss, unexplained aches or pain, periods of weeping and sadness, isolation and loneliness, and/or tension in relationships.

God was deeply troubled when He saw His creation spiraling into depravity and godlessness. God was so sorrowful about creating man that He decided to destroy the earth and everyone living on the earth. Instead of just acting immediately on that anger and sorrow, God looked for and found the good on earth in Noah. Even though God was sorrowful, He looked for something positive in the difficult situation and then provided a path of restoration for Noah, his family, and anyone else who would believe and go on the ark.

God allowed Noah 120 years to build the ark. His patience overrode His sorrow and anger. That is a perfect model of how we should approach sorrows. They should be short-term, and we should find the good in our situations and look for God's path of restoration out of it.

Jesus Had Sorrows

Jesus was deeply troubled... one of you will betray me.
(John 13:21)

The Last Supper was another perfect example of how to handle emotions in the midst of troubles. It was called "The Last Supper" because it was the last meal Jesus had with His disciples before His death. Jesus felt so many emotions that night. Judas would betray Him, and Peter would deny Him the next day. Yet what did Jesus do? He washed their feet.

What was Jesus's response to being deeply troubled and sorrowful? He responded to His hurt with love. Jesus felt a range of emotions. He was deeply troubled that one would betray Him, and one would deny Him. On the other hand, He felt tremendous love for His disciples all the way to the end.

Which emotion ruled the day? Jesus's love for His disciples overcame the grief He felt in His spirit. He could have been angry at Judas and thrown Him out of the house like God threw Adam and Eve out of the garden. He could have lashed out at Peter for being so weak and untrusting. Instead, He washed their feet and talked about love. Keep in mind that Jesus also knew that the next day He was going to suffer tremendous emotional, physical, and spiritual pain. Yet, He still responded in kindness and love.

Jesus Felt Tremendous Anguish

And being in anguish, he prayed more earnestly, and his sweat was like drops of blood falling to the ground. (Luke 22:44 NIV)

This was the night before the crucifixion. Jesus was in anguish! The definition of "anguish" is severe mental or physical pain or suffering. Being fully man as well as fully God, He felt the same emotions that you feel when you go through your troubles. Jesus was in so much emotional pain that His sweat became drops of blood falling to the ground.

Jesus suffered more on the cross than any normal human being could ever endure. He took all your emotional pain, sicknesses, and diseases, and all your sins upon Himself. He experienced the weight of that burden because He knew what was about to happen and was in agony. So, He prayed more earnestly.

In the midst of tremendous anguish, Jesus turned to the Father for comfort and as the anguish got more intense, He prayed harder. God heard His prayer and sent an angel to strengthen Him. Shortly after experiencing those intense emotions, Jesus was back to His old self and was instructing the disciples on how to handle grief.

> I tell you the truth, you will weep and mourn over what is going to happen to me, but the world will rejoice. You will grieve, but your grief will suddenly turn to wonderful joy. It will be like a woman suffering the pains of labor. When her child is born, her anguish gives way to joy because she has brought a new baby into the world. So you have sorrow now, but I will see you again; then you will rejoice, and no one can rob you of that joy. (John 16:20-22)

Jesus went from tremendous anguish to sudden, wonderful joy. He was about to go to the cross and He was at peace with His emotions. He said that the same thing was going to happen to them. They would weep and mourn when they saw Him die later that day. Jesus said that they would grieve. However, their grief would only be for a moment. "Suddenly" their grief would turn to wonderful joy.

Nothing is wrong with experiencing emotions, even agony. God gave feelings to us for a reason. However, sin has distorted the purpose of emotions. What we feel and how we act on those feelings is often nothing like what God intended. Consequently, emotions have become the source of great problems in our lives because they are no longer temporary.

There is supposed to be a time when the agony turns to joy. We are instructed by Scripture that it should only be one day. Jesus faced the greatest pain in the world, and it was only temporary. He was able to overcome it almost immediately. And He said He would give you that same ability. Over the next few days, you are going to learn how to turn emotional pain into joy almost immediately.

Emotions are Meant for Short-Term Present Reality

Sorrow, like anger, is only supposed to last for a moment. You were not designed to be depressed or to live in sorrow for days, months, or years. Your health and your body were not created to hold sorrow or anger for an extended period of time, and that is why it has been proven that depression, sorrow, grief, and emotional pain can cause long-term sickness and disease.

Things may happen in your life that create sadness or anger, and they may even cause you to weep bitterly. But God gave you instructions to release the pain the very next day and choose freedom. If you don't, then it will become a toxic emotion. Toxic emotions lead to sin which leads to devastating consequences.

A 2009 study of patients with severe chronic obstructive pulmonary disease found that twenty-two percent of the participants had at least mild depression. Several studies have shown that the outward expression of anger significantly increases risk of heart disease, diabetes, and other major diseases. A study found that anger was one of the "relative negative aspects" of women with eating disorders. Both anger and sorrow can become toxic and can even affect your health when they are not resolved immediately, preferably on the same day that you experience them.

Emotions were given to you by God to react to your present circumstances. This is important for you to understand because this will be the underlying theme of this book and the key to helping you feel free from all emotional pain that has led to bondage. Freedom is a present state of mind, but it is future focused. It relinquishes past chains or forms of bondage and allows for new hope, new life, and new beginnings to occur.

God and Jesus were perfect models of how to handle anger and sorrow. God does not experience time like we do. He's not always constantly dwelling on the past.

I, even I, am he who blots out your transgressions, for my own sake,
and remembers your sins no more.
(Isaiah 43:25 NIV)

Notice it says God forgets all about our past sins, for His sake, not ours, even though we are the beneficiary. It's for His benefit not to keep bringing up the past. He wants to deal with you in the present. If God let the accumulation of your sins determine how He would deal with you today, you would have no chance at an abundant life. His mercy and grace and ability to forget the past is what gives you the hope for the future.

When you are most like God, you are pressing forward, moving on, and growing in the likeness and image of your Creator. When you get stuck in an emotion, you are in a moment of separation from God's eternal movement. That's why emotions are only for present reality.

Emotions can be beneficial when they are used in that way. They are meant to deal with circumstances that are real or in the current moment. Remember that the root of the word "emotion" is to "move out."

Circumstances may happen that bring up anger and sorrow. God wants you to move them out of your life as quickly as possible. That's what God intended for emotions. Emotions are meant to be felt and then moved out of our lives. Depression, anxiety, bitterness, resentment, unforgiveness, fear, discontent, etc. are all emotions that are held in. That is not what God intended for you.

In the next chapter you're going to see how unresolved emotions multiply.

4

When Emotions Multiply

By definition, present reality emotions shouldn't be based on things that happened in your past or on the fear of something that might happen in the future. This is where the understanding of lasting freedom begins. It's the walk of faith when you allow God to handle your past as well as provide for your future. This leaves you living in your present reality dealing with difficult circumstances as they come. God even promised to be with you in those present troubles.

The Bible warns Christians that they will have many troubles. Life is full of danger, death, disease, and an enemy intent on destroying your life. No one is immune to going through present troubles. They are inevitable and you should emotionally prepare for them. It shouldn't be a surprise when troubles come into your life, and you should strive for the spiritual maturity to respond in faith so that your emotions stay under control.

Jesus said that we would face *many* trials and sorrows. It won't be a few. It will be a lot. The Greek word for *many* means often and numerous. The Greek word for *trials and sorrows* means tests. You're going to have many things happen to you that will either test your resolve and increase your perseverance or will create emotional pain and sorrow with the potential to act like a chain to your past.

You'll feel emotions when the troubles come. That's inevitable and normal. How you handle those emotions is a choice. Your emotional response will go a long way in determining how destructive those troubles are to your emotional well-being. At the same time, <u>the Bible tells us that God will never let us face a trial beyond what we are able to bear and that there is always a way out of the trial.</u>

While the Bible warns us that we will have many troubles, promises are attached to the verses:

"The Lord comes to the rescue each time."

"Take heart because I (Jesus) have overcome the world."

"The trial will not be more than you can bear."

"God will provide a way out so you can endure it."

Those are powerful promises that can soothe the pain and the duration of present troubles. It's comforting to know that God will never put more present troubles on you than what you can bear.

Jesus even said to take heart when you face troubles. "Take heart" means to not let your emotions get the best of you. It means to take control of your heart. The Bible says sin originates in your heart. It also says the heart is deceitful above all things.

Jesus was literally saying when troubles come, don't let your heart allow the troubles to create toxic emotions in you that cause you to sin. <u>Take control of your heart so it doesn't deceive you with false and painful emotions. You're not taking control of your heart when you allow it to dwell in emotions from the past or fear about the future.</u>

Take Heart Even in a Global Pandemic

At the time of this writing, we are in the throes of the coronavirus. That is a present trouble of global proportions. In the month after the disease first came to America, the use of anti-anxiety medications increased by 34.1 percent, according to a report released by pharmaceutical management company, Express Scripts.

Americans were already overmedicated. A Mayo Clinic study found that nearly 70 percent of Americans are prescribed at least one medication. The most commonly prescribed drugs are anxiety and antidepressant medications. The percentages are the same for Christians as non-Christians.

Many people turn to mood-altering medications to help them cope with their emotions. What they are feeling is too much to bear, so they need help to be able to temper the toxic feelings of anxiety and depression. Those statistics don't even account for those who turn to alcohol, illicit drugs, pornography, and other addictive behaviors to cope.

This part of the book is not in any way meant to make anyone feel guilty or shameful about taking medications. Many people need them to be able to cope with their circumstances. That's the point of this book. I'm not telling you to get off of them. People need them for a number of reasons, and you need to consider the advice of your physician. All I'm saying is that the promises in the Bible are clear: God will not put more on you than what you can bear emotionally on your own with His help.

If you have more emotional turmoil in your life than you can bear, then it's not because of your present troubles. If it were, that would be contrary to Scripture. Even in a global pandemic, you should not need to turn to medications to face the fear of it. A thirty-four percent increase in medications is anecdotal to the fact that a large percentage of people are not able to emotionally cope with the trauma of the virus.

Why are so many people experiencing emotions that are more than they can bear? It's because toxic emotions and troubles multiply.

When my anxious thoughts multiply within me...
(Psalm 94:19 NASB)

Troubles multiply for those who chase after other gods.
(Psalm 16:4)

Could this be the problem? Troubles don't add up to create emotional overload, they multiply. Two anxieties on top of two others is not four. It feels like twenty-four! I realize it's not an exact science, and we don't really know by how much they multiply, but I hope you get the point. Which is, our present troubles aren't creating the overload of emotions; the multiplication of unresolved troubles and emotions are.

What are the factors in the equation that are multiplying? They are: Past hurts. Present troubles, and Future Worries.

Past Hurts x Present Troubles x Future Worries = EMOTIONAL OVERLOAD

Past hurts make your present troubles worse. When past hurts are multiplied by future worries, when present troubles come, it becomes more than you can bear.

The Bible tells us in several verses that we are to forget the past and look forward to the hope of our future. The Apostle Paul said in order to focus on the future, you must forget the past. Remember, Paul had come out of a past life of murdering, torturing, and doing anything necessary to silence Christians. He was once filled with hate, anger, and an intense desire to destroy anything associated with Jesus and Christians.

He had a "freeing" moment on the road to Damascus when he met Jesus and was blinded by a light. At that moment and in the following days, he realized that he had wrongly murdered thousands of innocent Christians. Imagine the guilt, shame, and condemnation he must have felt when he came to that realization.

If anyone had a burden too great to bear, it should have been Paul. But he was emphatic in saying that his primary focus in life was forgetting the past. The Greek word for *focus* means to concentrate on, to emphasize, regulate, or control. It can also mean to funnel or converge attention into one direction. Forgetting the past and focusing on the future is similar to having tunnel vision which narrows your attention and blurs out peripheral distractions. You're concentrating on your future and forgetting your past by not allowing it into your vision or field of faith.

In an automobile, the windshield is many times larger than the rear-view mirror. Your focus when driving should primarily be on what's ahead of you. That's how God intended for you to live your life. You won't be a good driver if you're always looking in the rearview mirror and not focusing on the things ahead of you. Don't keep dwelling on your past. Your life will be filled with toxic emotions if you allow yourself to suffer from circumstances that aren't happening today.

March Madness is the annual NCAA basketball championship for college teams. In one particularly important game a few years ago, a player made a critical mistake at the end of the game that probably cost his team a chance to go to the Final Four and the opportunity to play for the National Championship. At the press conference after the game, he was crying and said, "I am going to think about this for the rest of my life." He may have just created an emotional root.

Emotional roots are created from difficult or traumatic circumstances from our past. Trained counselors search for these roots knowing that they may be the cause of emotional problems today, even though they may have happened years ago. Emotional roots are like weeds in your yard. The weed is what you see on the surface and is not attractive. However, the source of the weed is the root that has taken hold in the ground and supports the tentacles of the weed. In the same way, negative emotions you see on the surface are likely related to emotional roots deep within your soul.

Troubles Can Multiply

Not only can feelings multiply, but troubles can as well. Sometimes we bring the troubles on ourselves. Remember David. He was the one who said his anxiety and his troubles multiplied. He committed adultery with Bathsheba, and she became pregnant with his child. To cover up the sin, he had her husband killed. Then he denied the sin when confronted by the prophet. Because of his sin, his son died. What started as an affair, turned into a murderous scandal, and David paid a huge price.

Life has enough troubles of its own without adding to them our own sin and shortcomings. Look what David wrote about the emotional damage his past sin caused him to suffer in his present reality.

Because of your anger, my whole body is sick; my health is broken because of my sins. My guilt overwhelms me—it is a burden too heavy to bear. My wounds fester and stink because of my foolish sins. I am bent over and racked with pain. All day long I walk around filled with grief. A raging fever burns within me, and my health is broken. I am exhausted and completely crushed. My groans come from an anguished heart. You know what I long for, Lord; you hear my every sigh. My heart beats wildly, my strength fails, and I am going blind. My loved ones and friends stay away, fearing my disease. Even my own family stands at a distance. (Psalm 38:3-11)

David suffered the shame of his sin for years. The emotional pain of his past was overwhelming his present reality and destroying his life. It even affected his physical well-being. His whole body was sick. He was even going blind!

In later verses, David cried out in agony to God, asking, "Why am I discouraged? Why is my heart so sad?" Can you feel the angst in David's emotions? He described abandonment, grief, sorrow, oppression, ridicule, sickness, discouragement, loneliness, aimlessness, and sadness. He was what we would call today, a "basket case." Why did David have such toxic emotions? Look at the following timeline of his life and it is easy to see why he was so distressed. (We don't know David's exact ages when these events happened, but the below timeline will give you a general idea):

Event/Age

Father-in-law (Saul) tried to kill him.25

Father-in-law killed 85 of David's priests. 27

Hides for days in a cave. 27

Ziphites betrayed David. 28

Amalekites raided David's camp. 29

Had affair with Bathsheba. 50

Had her husband murdered. 50

Bathsheba pregnant, baby died. 50

David's son raped David's daughter. 53

Rapist son was killed by his brother. 53

Son Absalom tried to kill him. 56

Son Absalom was killed. 57

Famine in Israel. 59

Satan led David to take census. 68

70,000 people died because of David's sin. 68

No wonder David was such a mess. His father-in-law, Saul, who was the king, tried to kill him. David's own son tried to kill him. What emotions would you feel if the people close to you were trying to kill you. David fought countless wars. He won some and he lost

48

some. He won when he was trusting God and he lost when he turned his back on God.

The point is that he had plenty of troubles in his life. Some of his own doing and some were just the troubles of life. Most were not resolved when they happened and so they multiplied to the point that David felt like death.

Many of David's troubles were brought on himself by his own sin. Many times, troubles are not your fault. Do you remember the story of the woman with the issue of blood? The sickness was not her fault. Yet she had suffered for twelve whole years. Not that she didn't try to solve the trouble. It says that the woman spent "all she had" on doctors. Because of that, she was devastated financially. Her troubles magnified from health problems to also financial problems. That led to despair. Doctors had no idea how to treat the woman's blood disorder, so she was basically without hope. In fact, the Bible says things had gotten worse!

Many of your troubles are interrelated. Notice how one trouble can lead to another. Sickness, for example, can affect your finances. Financial worries can affect your marriage. Relationship problems can lead to addictions or chemical dependencies. Do you see the snowball effect your emotions can have on every area of life? It is important to keep your troubles from multiplying. They multiply when you allow your emotions to get out of control.

Experience Your Emotions in Real Time

Worrying about the future can make your current troubles worse. Worry is a debilitating emotion rooted in fear, which is the opposite of faith. Most people worry to some extent about their future. However, if you're not careful, you'll feel the actual emotions of potential future events even though they aren't happening in current reality.

That is when anxiety is birthed. The reality is you're anxious about something that's not real. Future troubles haven't happened yet. You'll face future troubles, but they may not be anything like what you're worrying about today. Even if they are, worrying about them today is a waste of time and energy. There's nothing you can do about them today, and worrying about them robs you of present-day joy, peace, and energy that could be better spent on family, and friends and solving your current troubles.

Paul said to forget the past; Jesus said not to worry about tomorrow. What's left is living in present reality. God promised He would not put more on you in your present reality than you can bear today. However, if you drag past hurts into today, your problems may be more than you can bear. If you are worried about tomorrow, which Jesus said not to do, then you may be dealing with more emotions than you can stand today.

The sad thing is that many people then blame God. They can't understand why God would let them go through so many bad things. They get mad at God because they are in so much pain. How can you blame God if you are allowing past hurts or future worries to overwhelm your present reality?

That's not His fault. If you believed the Scripture, then you would know it's true. Thinking God is somehow letting you down is a lie from the enemy that causes you to doubt Scripture. Just because you have more on you than you can bear doesn't mean that God put it there.

God's promises are always true, and the sooner you believe that the sooner you will feel free. If your emotions are overwhelming you to the point that you can't stand it anymore, then take a self-assessment. Are you hanging on to past hurts? Are you worrying about the future?

If you combine emotions from your past troubles with emotions you feel from today's troubles, and then add in emotions for troubles which may or may not happen in the future, it can create an overload of toxic emotions and can become too much to handle. In fact, it's not addition, it's multiplication. Emotions are like a virus. They multiply. It's no wonder so many people suffer from emotional and psychological disorders. Their systems are overloaded from dealing with past, present, and future troubles all at the same time.

Here's the great news. When you choose to live in current reality with faith in God, the past no longer controls you. You become strengthened by your experiences instead of manipulated by them. God created the human body to live free from shame, pain, regret, fear, and every other debilitating toxic emotion. We choose what we focus on. The Bible says that whatsoever things are good and lovely and of a good report, think on these things. That's a divine prescription for long-term emotional wellness.

It's no wonder so many people who suffer from emotional and psychological disorders, turn to doctors and are left to believe the only solution is chemically altering their brain with a pill. Their systems are overloaded from dealing with past, present, and future troubles all at the same time. Instead of dealing with the root of those toxic emotions, most people numb the pain through coping mechanisms like alcohol, drugs, sex, other vices, or medications.

Let's stop here and note there are many reasons why medical intervention may be necessary. You may be under a physician's care and taking medications right now to help you cope with your physiological or psychological needs. You may have been diagnosed with a disorder that requires immediate medical attention for the safety of your family or your own life. If that's the case, you should continue your treatment until you're completely healed and no longer in need of the medical help. God can use the treatment as a step in the process of healing you. <u>The goal, however, is to find the root of your</u> <u>issue and be completely whole again.</u>

It has become apparent through years of providing counseling to hundreds of individuals and couples that much of the medical intervention people use to fix symptoms wouldn't be necessary if emotions were based on present reality. The medications may improve the symptoms, but they aren't designed to heal the patient. They're designed to mask the symptoms to the point that he or she can bear them. God is about healing the patient. That's what this book is about as well.

Think about this though when you consider going on medication or you are evaluating why you need medication. An aspirin is a medication to help with a headache. Let me ask you this question: Do you need to take an aspirin for a headache you had two weeks ago? The obvious answer is no. Taking an aspirin today will have no effect on a headache you had in your past.

In the same way, do you need to take an aspirin today, for a headache you are going to have two weeks from now? Of course not. That defies all logic. Everyone knows that an aspirin will have no effect on a headache in your past or in your future.

So many people are on anxiety medicine and antidepressants because of things that happened in their past. Just as many people are on mood-altering medications because they are anxious about the future.

<u>If you'll focus on limiting your emotions to your present circum-</u> <u>stances, then the promises will manifest, and you will see healing.</u> <u>You won't face more than you can bear. You can rely on God's prom-</u> <u>ises and the fact that He is faithful. God promised that He'll deliver</u> <u>you from your troubles (Psalm 34:9). Jesus said He has overcome the</u> <u>troubles on your behalf (John 16:13).</u> God has assured us that He

won't allow more troubles than you can bear (1 Cor. 10:13). Limit your emotions to today, and you'll see those promises manifested in your life.

5

Jesus Made Emotional Freedom Possible

Years ago, a poor man purchased a ticket on a ship coming to America. He spent all he had to get the ticket and only had enough left to buy a few crackers and some cheese to last him the two weeks it would take to cross the ocean. Every day, the man would sit outside the dining room and watch all the other passengers indulge in the huge buffet of food available three times a day.

At the end of the voyage, the captain approached the man and asked, "Sir, have we done anything to offend you? I couldn't help but notice you never joined us in the dining room."

The man replied, "No. You haven't done anything to offend me. Everyone has been nice, and I've enjoyed my time on the ship."

The captain asked the man why he never joined them in the dining room. The man answered despondently, "I didn't have enough money to pay for the meals, so I just ate my cheese and crackers."

The captain passionately explained, "Sir, the meals were included in your ticket!"

In a similar way, most Christians aren't taking advantage of all the provisions Christ made for us on the cross. David implores us in Psalm 103:2 to "forget not all His benefits." Jesus, the night before His crucifixion, instituted the Lord's Supper and said to *remember* His body and blood. Meaning, His body broken for our sicknesses and His blood shed for the covering of our sins.

Forget not and remember are the same things. In this chapter, I want to emphatically remind you of the benefits of your salvation and what Jesus has done for you to make emotional freedom possible, so you'll never forget them. However, you must also remember that those benefits don't do you any good if you don't access them.

As I have explained in previous chapters, you will have troubles in this life. If you've lived long enough, you're already aware of that fact. When man sinned and fell short of the glory of God, he opened himself up to emotional pain, suffering, and troubles. The wages of sin is death. In other words, the consequences of sin are pain and suffering. Adam and Eve didn't have any troubles in the garden and didn't experience death. Someday, when we get to heaven there will be no more pain, suffering, or tears. Until that day comes, we need help coping with the troubles of this world.

That is why Jesus came to earth in the form of a man to provide redemption and help for our troubles. There are four categories of troubles or pain that you will experience in your lifetime. All toxic emotions can be tied to one of these four troubles. They are:

- Sin
- Sickness
- Sorrow
- Spiritual Attack

Every difficult situation you face in life will fall into one of these four categories. If you think back over your past troubles, you'll see it's true. However, did you realize Jesus has made a provision for every one of those troubles?

Sin: He himself bore our sins in his body on the cross (1 Peter 2:24 NIV).

Sickness: He took up our infirmities and bore our diseases (Matthew 8:17 NIV).

55

✳ Sorrow: Surely, He took up our pain and bore our suffering (Isaiah 53:4 NIV).

✳ Spiritual Attacks: But the Son of God came to destroy the works of the devil (1 John 3:8).

As you can see, God made a provision through Christ for every trouble you'll face. He "bore" your sins, sicknesses, and sorrows, and came to destroy every spiritual attack of the enemy. The word *bore* means to take up or to carry. Jesus literally took your sins, sicknesses, and sorrows upon Himself and carried them up to the cross.

Freedom from Sin

The Bible says that Jesus bore the punishment and was the propitiation for our sins. The word *propitiation* means to appease God. A one-time act, it redeemed us from any punishment from sin and made us right with God so that He would no longer punish us for our sins. If we confess and believe in Jesus, we are saved.

On the cross, Jesus Christ took away all your sin and made you right in God's sight. If you're right in God's sight, He's no longer mad at you. If He were, He'd have to apologize to Christ. Christ voluntarily took your sins and guilt upon Himself even though He was without sin. He sacrificed Himself so you could be in right standing with God.

Because you're in right standing with God, you can approach Him with confidence, not with guilt or always worried that He's going to punish you when you do something wrong. If Christ took your guilt, it would be unfair for God to make you feel guilty for your sins.

The pain caused from sin is a trouble in and of itself. Sin is the source of many of our toxic emotions. Having the knowledge of good and evil has left us with the realization our sin is evil, and the enemy would love for it to kill, steal, and destroy the abundant life we've been promised.

If you have the Holy Spirit living inside you, you'll be troubled by your sin. It'll make you suddenly feel uncomfortable. What you once thought to be "no big deal," will now seem unacceptable as the Holy Spirit brings conviction. If you choose to continue sinning, you'll begin to feel distant from the Father, and that's when the enemy creeps in to produce other symptoms. When left unaddressed in a Christian, sin produces the toxic emotions of guilt, shame, and condemnation. Those three emotions produce anxiety, depression, fear, anger, resentment, bitterness, and all sorts of negative emotions.

David said, several times in the Psalms, that his sin troubled him. He confessed his sin, but he was still emotionally troubled by it. He didn't have the benefit of the new covenant of grace with the provision Christ made for sin. You don't have to be troubled indefinitely by your sin because it's covered by the blood of Jesus. He took your sins and paid the penalty for them on the cross.

David was perhaps the greatest narcissist of all time. He was prideful, entitled, selfish, demanding, lacking empathy, deceptive, controlling, and had no sense of remorse when committing such grave sins. But despite his deep, dark secrets, when he came before God in humility and repentance, God forgave him and didn't require death for his or Bathsheba's trespass. Nevertheless, their baby died, and David experienced tremendous pain as he struggled through the resolution of this major sin in his life. Here are some of David's writings about his sin and the emotional pain it caused him:

When I refused to confess my sin, my body wasted away, and
I groaned all day long. Day and night your hand of discipline was
heavy on me. My strength evaporated like water in the summer heat.
(Psalm 32:3-4)

David said his refusal to confess his sin was having a physical effect on his body. He groaned all day long. Despair caused him pain, all day and all night. He could never get relief from the agony of his sin. He was so consumed with guilt, shame, and condemnation, it was destroying his life.

The above verses clearly show the effect of the knowledge of good and evil on emotions. David said he was in despair years later from sins he'd committed in his past. That's why it's important to receive the forgiveness of your sins through Christ's finished works on the cross. You already know what you've done that is sinful and evil. That's the knowledge of good and evil manifesting in your life and producing negative emotions.

David did not have the benefit of Christ's propitiation for his sins on the cross. You do. You can be free from the emotional fallout from your sins. You no longer live under the old covenant. You don't have to agonize over your sins for decades like David did. You can choose freedom by recognizing that your sins were nailed to the cross, and the burden of sin and death are no longer yours to carry.

The Bible even says that God forgets your sins. What a powerful, freeing truth, if you will believe it. God forgives you because of Christ, and don't ever forget it!

Forgetting is a choice. God has chosen not to remember your sins anymore, so why should you? Even if the enemy tries to remind you of your past mistakes or failures, you can resist those thoughts and voices and refuse to allow them to take root in your current emotions. God said your sins are forgiven through the blood of Christ.

That is your present reality.

Freedom from Sickness

Sickness can negatively affect your emotions. Toxic emotions can also negatively affect your health and produce sicknesses. Research has proven that the symptoms of illness we feel in our bodies are directly connected to our emotional wellbeing and vice-versa. Do you see the vicious cycle? When your emotions are causing you pain, your physical body suffers. If your body is sick, your emotions can turn toxic. If your emotions are toxic, any kind of trouble can put you over the edge of emotional stability. That's why identifying the root issues of your current emotions is so vital to your overall wholeness.

By continuing to look at the life of King David, we can see the intense impact emotions can have on one's overall health. We can also see that sin often leads to emotional instability which can also lead to physical sickness.

I've seen many people over the years who were sick because of their emotions or at least their physical infirmities were made worse by their toxic emotions. It's well documented that physical addictions such as alcoholism and drug abuse create diseases. We've rarely seen a physical addiction that didn't have an emotional root.

Do you remember the woman with the issue of blood from the last chapter? She suffered for twelve years and had lost hope. To make things worse, society had labeled her "unclean." In Biblical times, if you were unclean, you couldn't go into the public without declaring "I am unclean. I am unclean." If this woman failed to declare her state of uncleanliness, she could be stoned to death. If anyone were to touch her, they became unclean as well and would have to isolate from the rest of society.

Can you imagine the shame this must have caused her? She likely had been abandoned by her friends and family, and it had probably been years since anyone had touched her. She wasn't allowed in the Temple, so she probably even felt abandoned by God.

Yet a miraculous thing happened to her. She met Jesus. She saw Him walking down the road. A crowd was around Him, causing quite a commotion. Something inside her prompted her to rush to Him and touch His garment. She believed that if she did, then she would be healed. What tremendous faith!

That is exactly what happened. She touched His garment, the disease immediately left her body, and the Bible says she was made whole. The word *whole* means complete, intact. Like a loaf of bread is whole when it first comes out of the oven. Her broken body was now intact.

God wants emotional wholeness for you as well! It's God's desire that you be in health, physically, and emotionally. God wants your physical health to prosper along with your soul which is where your emotional well-being dwells. You can't effectively do it on your own strength. Medication can help, but it's not the cure. The cure is believing that Christ has borne your sin and sickness, believing it by faith and then receiving it by refusing to be troubled emotionally by it.

Sorrows Should Have an Expiration Date

Companies often put expiration dates on their products. When they take an inventory, they want to make sure nothing is past its expiration date. If it is, then it should be thrown out. If something is nearing its expiration, they'll usually discount the price and try to move it out of their inventory before it goes bad. The consumer is instructed to throw out any product that is past its expiration date because it may harm him.

In the same way, God has set clear expiration dates on your emotions. You need to experience your emotions based on God's time frame, not based on how long you want to suffer. If you do that, your suffering will be short-term. You may think that's not realistic. You probably have never realized you can control your emotions to that extent. However, you can refuse to be comforted by God during troubles. Notice how David refused to be comforted, so his sorrows lasted indefinitely.

> In the day of my trouble I sought the Lord; My hand was stretched out in the night without ceasing; My soul refused to be comforted.
> (Psalm 77:2 NKJV)

David said he sought the Lord in his times of trouble. God wanted to comfort him in his time of trouble, yet he refused to be comforted by the Lord. As we have seen previously, Jesus "bore" our sorrows. In other words, He carried them. We can never change the fact that He bore our sorrows, but we can refuse to be comforted by that fact.

Grief and sorrows can surface for any number of reasons. They usually come from loss. The death of a loved one, divorce, broken relationships, bankruptcy, theft, persecution, or other losses can create tremendous emotional pain. So, how can we experience such deep loss and realistically expect the sorrow to be temporary? Doesn't grief or the death of a loved one take time to heal? Is it something you ever really get over?"

Those are good questions. The present truth is that the person is no longer with you and you miss them. The void is real. It hurts and can even feel like the wind has been knocked out of your sails. However, the Bible says there is supposed to be a specific time frame for mourning, so it prevents us from suffering further pain, sickness, and distress. Like Ecclesiastes 3:4 says, there should be a specific time when the mourning begins and a set time frame for when it is over.

The Psalmist said that God can restore your joy by the next morning!

Your suffering is only supposed to be short-term, and God Himself will restore you and make you strong, firm, and steadfast. While you may have troubles that create suffering and sorrows, they're supposed to be temporary. We are told to remain steadfast when we face trials. The definition of *steadfast* is firm, unshakable, and unwavering. If you refuse to be comforted, you'll be weak, shaky, and wavering. God wants to use the troubles you face to transform you into a strong and mighty warrior with unshakable faith.

> He comforts us in all our troubles so that we can comfort others.
> When they are troubled, we will be able to give them the same
> comfort God has given us. For the more we suffer for Christ, the
> more God will shower us with his comfort through Christ.
> (2 Corinthians 1:4-5)

The more troubles you have, the more comfort God provides you through Christ. Notice it says he comforts you in "all" troubles. You won't face a single trouble that God won't comfort you through. He comforts you so you can be a comfort to others when they face troubles.

If you refuse to be comforted, then you'll deal with the pain and suffering indefinitely. In addition, you won't be any use to others who need comfort in their troubles. Further, you'll miss out on the heavenly shower of God's comfort.

You Don't have to be Afraid of Spiritual Attacks

The battle for your emotional health is really a battle against an enemy who wants to destroy you by keeping you in bondage to toxic emotions. Jesus said the thief (Satan) comes to steal, kill, and destroy. He does this by sending troubles into your life to create havoc, pain, and emotional bondage. Your battle is not against people, companies, or even God. The battle you're facing is a spiritual war that God has already assured you, He has won on your behalf.

Our primary battle is not with flesh and blood but with evil spirits. The battle for your emotions is a spiritual war, waged in your soul. If Satan can get you to stay bound to your negative emotions, he knows you'll be impotent in the things of God. Even when it seems like you're fighting a physical family member or a person creating conflict in your life, you're actually in a battle against the enemy and his forces.

This is why Satan isn't satisfied with giving you only one trouble. He wants to give you as many troubles as he can, with the intent to destroy every area of your life. Ultimately, he knows if he can bring enough trouble against God's people, he may influence them to turn their back on God altogether.

In the book of Job, God gave Satan permission to test Job's faith. Satan didn't give Job just one trouble. Job was a wealthy man, and Satan destroyed his finances. Satan killed Job's seven sons and three daughters with a mighty wind. If that wasn't bad enough, Satan afflicted Job with horrible and painful sores all over his body. Every area of Job's life was attacked by Satan whose goal was to get Job to curse God. Imagine the emotions Job felt, having lost everything dear to him.

Multiple spiritual attacks can create overwhelming emotions. Job's suffering was "too great for words." Have you ever been so low that words couldn't express how much you were suffering? When you lose something of value, it creates emotional pain. That's why Satan tries to steal and destroy things valuable to you. Satan hates God. God has blessed you, and Satan wants to steal your blessings. What he really wants is for you to turn away from God. He knows the best way to hurt God is to hurt you. It hurts God more when you blame Him for your suffering and succumb to the lies of the enemy.

In Job 1:22, the Bible says, "In all of this, Job did not sin by blaming God." Don't blame God for your troubles. The Bible says every good and perfect gift comes from God (James 1:17). You must recognize your troubles aren't sent by God; they're from your enemy. God does, however, allow you to face troubles so the testing of your faith will strengthen you and develop perseverance. If you see God as the "sender" of troubles, you'll be tempted to blame God for your current circumstances instead of seeing Him as your deliverer. Resist the thoughts that God is behind your troubles. That will only make things worse.

You will be attacked. It is inevitable. You cannot prevent the spiritual attacks any more than you can escape the many troubles Jesus said you would have. It's normal to feel afraid when you're under attack. However, it's supposed to be a temporary emotion. You can be confident in knowing that you don't have to be afraid. Whatever negative emotion you feel at the time of the attack can be turned to confidence immediately as you let God take control of your emotions.

The Bible recounts a time when Jesus met a woman named Mary Magdalene. Who was Mary? She helped finance Jesus's ministry. She was present at the cross and at the tomb when Jesus was resurrected. It wasn't that way when Jesus met her. Mary was tormented by evil spirits for years. Jesus cast out the demons, Mary was saved and became an important part of His ministry.

In another instance, Jesus encountered a woman who had been under spiritual attack for eighteen years!

Jesus asked, "Isn't it right that she be released?" That was right after he healed the woman who'd been crippled for eighteen years by an evil spirit.

Ask yourself the same question: Isn't it right that you be released from the physical and emotional pain you've suffered? Yes! A thousand times yes!

You don't have to experience long-term emotions from spiritual attacks. Jesus was well aware of the fact that you would experience spiritual attacks in your life. He came to destroy those works. That should give you hope and the power to overcome the negative emotions that are inevitably present from spiritual attacks.

The above stories were real people facing real spiritual attacks. Their troubles were real and devastating. Their emotions were real as well, and they suffered from them. However, notice God moved in every situation. David was delivered from his enemies, time and time again. Saul tried to kill him on numerous occasions, but Saul is the one who died at the hands of his enemies. The woman with the demons was completely healed. Mary Magdalene became a mighty woman of God.

God hasn't forgotten your struggles either. God has your back. He's not going to let Satan attack you without making a provision to protect you from the attack. You may not know how or when the provision will come, but you can know it will because of the promises of God if you believe by faith that God will provide for you.

In the next two chapters, I'm going to talk about how to reset your emotions so that you can overcome them and the evil one.

6

Invalidate Your Feelings

For several years, my wife and I fostered rescue dogs. They were dogs that came from difficult situations, usually with a lot of fears and emotional problems. Our job was to teach them the skills to become good pets and to help them overcome their fears. One of the first things we did was to get them comfortable on a leash and take them for daily walks downtown. This taught them discipline and gave them much needed exercise to work out their anxieties. The key was getting them to trust us as soon as possible.

Downtown was a good place to walk to help them overcome their fears because there were a lot of people and noises to confront. One of our fosters was a goldendoodle named Dallas who learned to walk on the leash but was afraid of loud noises. He cowered when ambulances, motorcycles, and large trucks drove by or anyone made a sudden movement.

What he didn't know was that he was perfectly safe and that we would never let anything hurt him. He didn't have to be afraid of those noises because he could trust us to protect him. If he really knew that we would keep him safe, then he wouldn't worry about the loud noises, no matter how scary they seemed.

That is probably similar to how God looks at us when our feelings are out of control. If we really believe that God will keep us safe, then we would fully trust Him and not be afraid. Fear, worry, and anxiety are really mistrust in God. As foster parents, we had to get Dallas to realize he could trust us. You have to know you can trust

God and then believe it by faith. When you do, the feelings become manageable.

We have two toy poodles of our own who we rescued several years ago. One weighs six pounds, the other seven. One day we were walking them downtown when we suddenly heard this blood-curdling scream. A young girl, who appeared to be about five or six-years-old, was crying and cowering in fear behind her mother. She had seen our dogs and was petrified. We quickly moved past them, but I could still hear her crying almost a block away.

Even though her fear was real, it wasn't based in reality. Our dogs would not and could not hurt her. If anything, she could hurt them a lot worse than they could hurt her. Yet, the feeling was so overwhelming that it had overcome her present reality and caused her to respond in an irrational way.

That is an important truth to learn. Even though you feel something, that doesn't mean it's real. Just because you believe something, that doesn't make it true. Therefore, all feelings and thoughts must be tested based on present reality.

In 1990, a self-proclaimed climatologist named Iben Browning predicted a major earthquake to strike St. Louis on December 3, give or take a few days. The prediction caught the attention of the national media and hysteria broke out in the region, and the country became riveted to what was going to be a major catastrophe.

The Federal Emergency Management Agency added to the hysteria when they projected that the bridges across the Mississippi River would collapse, that a third of buildings as far away as Chicago would be affected, and twenty-one states and fifteen million people would be affected. Some "experts" speculated that the Mississippi River would widen and destroy towns and homes from St. Louis all the way to New Orleans, creating a huge divide in the center of the country.

Some were saying it would be the worst catastrophe in American history. Schools were closed and thousands fled the area. I had an employee in my company who was supposed to travel to St. Louis on business that week. She was so afraid of the prediction that the trip had to be cancelled.

Thirty years later, we are still waiting for the earthquake to happen.

Feelings Come from Thoughts

Search me, O God, and know my heart; test me and know my
anxious thoughts.
(Psalm 139:23 NIV)

Anxiety is birthed from wrong thoughts. The above verse says that anxious thoughts come out of your heart. Feelings do not exist in a vacuum. They originate somewhere. The source of toxic feelings are thoughts not grounded in present reality that originate from the heart.

If you control your thoughts, you control your feelings. Feelings lead to actions. Negative feelings lead to negative actions. Really, negative thoughts lead to negative feelings, which lead to negative actions. When I am counseling someone, who is acting in a way that is destructive or irrational, I don't focus on the behavior or their feelings. I focus on the thoughts that lead to the feelings that lead to the destructive behavior. Every negative emotion has an underlying thought. Identify the thought, change the thought from negative to positive, and the feelings will change, and the behavior will follow.

The problem with most "lost" people in the world is that they are controlled by their feelings and, more often than not, those feelings are irrational. That's why there is so much destructive behavior coming from those living in the world without Christ. Unfortunately, most Christians have conformed to the pattern of the world and let their feelings and thoughts control their actions. The result is there is little difference between the behaviors of the world and the behaviors of Christians who have been redeemed from the world. The ultimate result is the erosion of the moral fabric of the society.

That's why it's so dangerous to follow your feelings or emotions, especially when they are rooted in your past or based on a future worry. Feelings cannot be trusted. You can easily make bad decisions when you are following your feelings. People end their marriages over wrong feelings. People have affairs because they are following their hearts. People turn away from God because they wrongly accuse Him of causing their afflictions. Feelings can't be trusted when they are not from God.

If thoughts and feelings are contrary to the Word of God, they come from wrong beliefs. If your thinking is wrong, your feelings will be wrong, and if you follow those feelings, you will get outside of God's will for your life.

Where do thoughts come from? They come from beliefs. Look at the following pattern:

1. Wrong beliefs lead to wrong thoughts.
2. Wrong thoughts lead to negative feelings.
3. Negative feelings, if allowed to become toxic, lead to destructive actions.

All destructive actions can be traced back to a wrong belief. Those wrong beliefs originate in your heart. Have you ever heard the expression "You need to follow your heart?" Look at what the Bible says about following your heart:

> The heart is deceitful above all things, And desperately wicked;
> Who can know it?
> (Jeremiah 17:9 KJV)

Read what Jesus said about the heart:

For out of the heart proceed evil thoughts, murders, adulteries, fornications, thefts, false witness, blasphemies.
(Matthew 15:19 NKJV)

Jesus said evil thoughts lead to murders! Adulteries! Blasphemies!
If you follow your heart, it will lead you to destruction.

There is a way that seems right to a man, But its end is the
way of death. (Proverbs 14:12 NKJV)

You can't trust your feelings to lead you in the right direction.
Feelings aren't always based on reality and certainly aren't always
based on God's will for your life. They may seem right at the time,
but they lead to death. If our enemy can manipulate your thoughts
and your feelings, he can get you to do things that will destroy your
life.

Most people in the world marry or enter into romantic entangle-
ments because of feelings. Romantic relationships based on feelings
will likely end in divorce because feelings don't last. Remember, feelings are meant for present reality. When present reality changes, and
you no longer have the feelings, then you are tricked into believing
that you are no longer in love with that person, and you end the
marriage.

I've seen the pattern hundreds of times. Often, a person will find
someone else who renews feelings of love that is missing in their
marriage, and they have an affair. That is why more than fifty percent of married couples have an affair. Many leave their spouse for
the new relationship. Yet more than ninety-seven percent of relationships that start from an affair end in divorce! Why is that? Because the feelings will eventually fade. That is the nature of feelings.
They are not designed to last.

Because feelings were created in us by God for immediate present reality, feelings change as often as our present reality changes. What you feel today, you are unlikely to feel for the rest of your life. That's why making lifetime decisions on feelings is dangerous. You just can't trust them to last.

Have you ever watched an episode of the Bachelor or Bachelorette? The contestants are living out this principle for the world to see in real time. One minute, they are pledging their undying love to another contestant. In the same episode, they get engaged to a different contestant. How is that possible? One study found that only four of the first twenty-four couples who got engaged on the show are actually still together.

When you live your life based on feelings, you will make poor decisions. Feelings not based on present reality and grounded beliefs will lead you astray almost every time. You can't trust them.

What can you trust? You can trust the Word of God. God never changes. His Word never changes. He is the same yesterday, today and forever. He is not controlled by feelings that change every day. God and His Word are realities that you can count on all the time regardless of how you feel. The answer to not acting on your feelings is to change your thoughts to align with the Word of God.

You are not to act and make decisions in the same way the world does. You are to be transformed by the renewing of your mind. In other words, you need to change your thoughts so that you can prove that your thoughts and feelings are the good and acceptable and perfect will of God. If you really take the time to do that mental and spiritual exploration, you may find that your feelings don't line up with God's Word and are not the will of God. That will keep you from making a tragic mistake that can ruin your life.

Your heart needs to be transformed before you can count on it. The word *transformed* in Romans 12:2, gets my attention. Any verse that talks about a transformation should get you excited. It should make you want to take notice and get motivated on how to receive that transformation. The Greek word for transformation is *metamorphoo*, which is where we get the word metamorphosis. It means a total change from the inside out. That is what we need in our feelings. A total transformation.

How Do You Renew Your Mind?

You can change your feelings at any time by changing the wrong beliefs behind the feelings. That is a powerful truth that will change your life. The emotional battlefield is in the mind. That's why many of the counseling strategies in the world that try to help people change their feelings without changing the underlying beliefs don't work. If you don't change the underlying false belief, then the feelings will never be completely gone.

Here's how it works: A lady had ended an adulterous relationship that was really bad for her. She was having a hard time getting over the feelings. Months later she was still struggling with the feelings. She kept thinking, "I want to get over him, but I just can't. Why won't the feelings go away?" She kept saying out loud, "I still have feelings for him. I can't get over him. Why did I like him so much?"

She desperately wanted to not feel that way anymore and didn't understand why she still had those unwanted feelings. In reality, each time she said, "I still have feelings for him, why won't they go away," she was reinforcing the feelings by having the thoughts.

Occasionally, she would run into him, and seeing him made it harder to get over the feelings. The feelings were fading over time, which they generally do, and she was never going to become involved with him again, but as long as the thoughts were there, the

Invalidate Your Feelings

feelings would not go away completely. The thoughts were giving life to the feelings.

One day she ran into him and they had a conversation. He said something that made her mad. She walked away from him in mid sentence and said to herself, "I am so over him." The feelings immediately went away. Instantly! What was the difference? The change was in her thinking. As long as she kept thinking she had feelings for him, then she did. As long as she kept saying that she couldn't get over the feelings, then she couldn't.

The moment she changed her thinking and said to herself that she was over him, the feelings followed the thoughts. She never had those feelings again. A few weeks later, she learned that he was telling people lies about her, and the feelings turned to disdain. Now her thinking has changed to "He's a liar. He is not a good person. He is trying to hurt me." The feelings were now disdain and mistrust. How she felt about him was totally related to what she thought about him.

Interrupt Your Thoughts

Try this. For ten seconds, think about a pink elephant. Now, for ten seconds think about a purple cow. I just changed what you are thinking by suggestion. Now, for ten seconds don't think about a pink elephant. Now, for ten seconds don't think about a purple cow. Were you able to do it? No matter how hard you try, you will still think about the elephant and the cow, unless you do something to change your thoughts. Even if you are telling yourself not to think about them. If you distract yourself from thinking about them, then you can successfully change your thoughts. If you distract yourself from your negative thoughts, you can successfully change them as well.

Now, try this. Silently, count to ten. When you get to five, say your name out loud. What happened? You quit counting to ten. Why? Because speaking changes your thoughts. That is how you change your feelings. You cannot think about something negative when you are speaking something totally different.

Many years ago, I was a worship leader at a large church in Fort Worth, Texas. I had a member of our worship team who would get really nervous before the service. She kept saying out loud, "I am so nervous." The more times she said it, the more nervous she felt. Feelings come from thoughts and they are reinforced by spoken words. I suggested to her that she change her words. Instead of saying that she was nervous, she should say, "I am so excited to be on the worship team today." Eventually, the nervousness changed to excitement.

What should you speak? God's Word. Say Scriptures out loud, when you are having negative thoughts and feelings. The spoken word will provide temporary relief. Ultimately, you have to change the wrong beliefs in order for the feelings to go away completely. The first step to changing the wrong beliefs is to realize that they are a lie.

Counterfeit Emotional Pain

Several years ago, I was working with an individual who was in intense emotional pain. She described the words someone had spoken to her that day that were hurtful and had plunged her into a severe depression. The pain was so intense she was almost in a fetal position and could barely talk because of her deep sobbing.

As I talked to her, the Holy Spirit showed me that the pain was not real. The enemy had manufactured it. It felt real, but it wasn't. I told her what the Holy Spirit told me, and she looked at me like I was crazy. I laid my hand on her shoulder and prayed the following prayer: "I command that the pain and depression you are feeling right now must leave your body in the name of Jesus." Immediately, she stopped crying, sat up straight, and the pain was almost completely gone. Within an hour, it was totally gone, and she was filled with joy and happiness that God had healed her.

I'm not saying that every pain or sickness or emotional hurt is not real. Real circumstances do happen in our lives that create emotional pain and sorrow. What I'm saying is that there is a worldly sorrow that leads to pain that's not real. So much of what we experience is not based on present reality.

For instance, movies, TV shows, songs, and other entertainment mediums all try to create an emotional response from the audience. I've seen people cry when a character on a movie or television show dies. That sorrow is not real. It feels real but it is not based on any reality. A real death in the family causes sorrow and grief. A death of a character who doesn't exist other than in the imagination of the creator and writer is not a real sorrow that should affect your emotions. In fact, it is the enemy's plan. If Christ died for all our emotional pain and suffering, it makes sense that the enemy would try to get us to feel emotional pain and suffering at every opportunity.

I don't watch horror movies. I don't want to reinforce feelings of fear. The Bible says to "fear not" three hundred and sixty-five times. Why would I want to try and manufacture fear that is not based on reality? You should be careful what counterfeit emotions you let into your life.

Disown Your Feelings

The Bible tells us to **get** rid of toxic emotions. The word *get* means to cause something to happen. To "get rid" of something means to cause it to be removed or uprooted. It's like throwing out the trash or doing a spring cleaning and getting rid of unwanted things that are cluttering your house.

The verse "Don't let the sun go down on your anger," teaches us how to keep our emotions in present reality. It shows the importance of releasing outdated feelings and to stop giving Satan an inroad into our emotions. We've already learned anger is supposed to be dealt with the same day someone makes you angry. If the anger controls you and you let the anger linger beyond one day, the anger gives the devil an opportunity to create a foothold in your life.

The Greek word for *foothold* means an inhabited place. Unresolved emotions are an invitation to the devil to set up an inhabited place in your soul. A foothold is the same as an emotional root. An emotional root or a foothold literally allows Satan to take up residence in your soul.

You need to "get" rid of all the dwelling places of Satan in your soul. Remember, your body is the Temple of the Holy Spirit. It's your house. It's also God's house. Your body is a house where God resides. Satan has no business setting up an inhabited place in your body. Get rid of his dwelling places. You need to take the bulldozer (Holy Spirit) and let him destroy and remove all your unwanted emotional roots.

That's why we tell you to disown your feelings. The world will tell you that you must own your emotions. They tell you to "be true to your feelings." Many people even create their belief system around how they feel or what emotions govern them most at the moment. But choosing to be led by your emotions is like walking down a path of destruction.

Satan's playground is the emotional roots of past experiences. He lives there. He wants you to stay in that playground forever. His goal is to convince you that your past is an excuse for harboring bitter roots in your future. Don't partner with his manipulation. Don't joint-venture or cohabitate with the enemy. Disown those old, outdated emotions, and let Christ be the only force dwelling in your temple.

Psychologists tell us to own our emotions. I am telling you the opposite. Don't own emotions that aren't based on reality. Don't own emotions based on lies from the enemy. Do the opposite: disown your negative emotions. Refuse to accept emotions not based on present reality. You must reject the memories of your past and future worries that can't be based on reality because they haven't happened yet.

The Bible says not to dwell on the past. The word *dwell* means to live or linger in. Memories cause us to live in the past. Negative memories are a tool Satan uses to create ongoing pain from the circumstances in your past. Once you have a trouble in your life, Satan takes the emotions you feel in that trouble and recreates them over and over again through memories. They are images or videos you continually replay like an old movie reel. You reinforce those memories with the words you speak. "I will never get over this. I will never forget what you did to me." Those words establish and reinforce emotional roots.

A couple came in for counseling due to the fallout from an affair. When they first sought counsel, they were separated and headed for divorce. After a few weeks of digging deeper into their story and timelines, they began to see the enemy's goal to kill, steal, and destroy their family and unity. Soon, they moved back in together and were reestablishing their relationship. God did a miracle in their marriage.

However, as time passed, the wife kept playing movies of her husband's affair in her head. She imagined the conversations. She pictured the sex and tried to imagine their feelings for each other. Haunted by those memories, they were causing her deep emotional pain. The result was lashing out at her husband and reminding him of his past failures. Every time she played the movie of his affair in her mind, she grew angrier.

Finally, she came back for more counseling to find out how to get over the memories. Both she and her husband wanted to move forward in their marriage, but as long as she was playing the movie in her head, she was allowing the stronghold or old emotional root to sabotage their future.

By helping her see that those outdated memories weren't real, and the affair was no longer happening, she began to realize her emotions weren't based on present reality. The current truth was that her husband loved her, and he was now faithful to her and their marriage. The solution to their situation was for her to focus on the future hope and the current love they now had together.

The future for their family was bright, and forgiveness was the key to her freedom. We told her, "You are the writer and director of the movie that plays in your head, so change the script. As soon as the movie starts playing old memories, picture your husband telling the woman, 'I can't do this. I love my wife. I love God and I want to serve God.' Picture him telling the woman he'll never see her again. Hear him say to her that he is committed to you and loves you deeply. Imagine him telling her the affair is over for good. Picture your husband walking out of the room and coming to you and telling you how much he loves you and is committed to you. Picture forgiving him and welcoming him back with open arms. Picture him embracing and making love to you."

Fictional movies are a tactic of the enemy. He wants you to play these outdated memory reels, so you feel the pain over and over again. When you let Satan direct the script of your emotions, you'll suffer. If you play God's movie, which is real and based on truth, you can redeem the situation and move forward in the newness of life.

Once a foothold is established, Satan can play those memories anytime he wants, and then he has gained control of your emotions.

Have you ever heard anyone say, "He knows how to push my buttons?" They may be talking about another person, but they'd be more accurate by saying Satan knows how to push your buttons.

Buttons are emotional roots and footholds. Satan is the one manipulating those emotions from his residence in your soul. Once a foothold is established, Satan can make you feel those negative emotions anytime he wants. These are called triggers. Most people think the triggers come from the outside. Triggers are actually inside you, and Satan is the one pulling the trigger to make you feel the negative emotion. You are directing your anger at the wrong person. You should be directing it toward the enemy within.

Reject Thoughts from the Enemy

I've talked a lot about David in this book. One of the major mistakes David made in his life was when he took a census of the people. God was so angry that David paid a horrible price for his sin. Where did he get the idea? The Bible says that Satan put the thought in his head. Right before Judas Iscariot betrayed Christ, the Bible says that Satan entered his heart. Sometimes thoughts and feelings come from the enemy. When we act on them, death and destruction is the result.

Satan can't enter into a Christian without his permission. However, he will enter any open door. Judas was greedy and opened the door to thoughts of sin. The thought to betray Jesus for money came from the enemy. The thought had no power until Judas considered acting on it. Once he acted on it, he opened the door to destruction.

When Judas realized what he'd done, he became so distraught he killed himself. That's the kind of thing that happens when you give the enemy an opportunity. He'll take that opening and run with it as far as you'll let him. He'll lead you all the way to death if you allow him to and will inflict great emotional pain along the way. That should tell you a lot about Satan. He used Judas to betray Jesus. Rather than rewarding him, he destroyed his life by getting him to commit suicide.

David had the thought to conduct a census. God told him not to do it. He did it anyway and 70,000 of his priests died. Imagine if one of your thoughts led to the death of 70,000 people! Your thoughts and feelings that are not from God have the same potential to destroy your life. You are not the king of the world and 70,000 people might not be affected, but those around you can be.

You can make decisions based on feelings and thoughts that can have devastating consequences to those around you. Every decision made from a transformed mind will result in peace and good outcomes. Not everything will always go perfectly, but God will always work everything together for our good if we love Him and continue to seek Him.

Feelings and thoughts that are contrary to the Word of God should be discarded from your life like trash. Disown them. Invalidate them. The word *invalidate* means to prove to be false. Put your thoughts and feelings on trial. Find out if they are true or false. If they are false, then don't give them any place in your life.

7

System Reset

Your computer has a feature that allows it to be restored back to its original factory settings. It's called a system reset or a system restore. When you first get a new computer, it's free from bugs, viruses, or glitches. After continued use, corrupted files can infiltrate the system and cause the computer to function at less than optimum. If the computer is damaged too badly, a factory reset might be necessary to restore the computer to its original state.

In a similar way, man was perfect in his original setting in the Garden of Eden, but sin corrupted his systems. Adam and Eve's lives in the garden were perfect in every way. Their emotions were only positive feelings of peace and joy. They had no inhibitions, no sins, no lust, no arguments, no pain, no sorrows, no suffering, no strife, no worries, no anxieties, no fears, and no depression. They always responded with perfect emotions just like God.

Then sin entered the world and so did all the emotional consequences of sin. Man's emotions became corrupted, much like a virus corrupts a computer system. Over time, troubles can inevitably corrupt your emotions. The worries of this life, deceitfulness, lusts of the flesh, and desires for things that aren't of God get inside your mind and create feelings of pain and suffering. Sin was the original virus that corrupted your emotional system, and ongoing troubles have choked off the word and made life unfruitful for many.

Computer viruses are very destructive and can cause permanent damage when they embed themselves into the internal structure of the device. The viruses lock into the memory so they can keep running in the background wreaking havoc on the health of the computer. That's exactly what toxic emotions do to you. They attach themselves into your soul through memories, embedding themselves into the deep recesses of your mind and soul. They keep running in the background and corrupt your everyday life, hindering your ability to function properly.

In some cases, viruses lock computers down so that they can't even function. In the same way, Christians can become so overloaded with emotions they have emotional breakdowns. While not always debilitating, so many toxic memories and emotions infect people so that they are not able to function at optimum in their everyday lives. They are "damaged goods" so to speak.

Maintaining normal relationships becomes a struggle. The slightest trouble will set them into emotional turmoil. They are quick to anger and/or cry themselves to sleep at night. They lash out at those who love them and want to help. The end result is they often turn away from God and abandon the church, isolating themselves from those who can offer support. When it gets to that point, they often turn to medications, drugs, alcohol, illicit sexual relationships, or other destructive behaviors, or become so embittered that they shut down altogether emotionally.

We All Need a Factory Reset

Everyone needs a system reset of the soul, which includes our emotions. To do this, we must go back to our manufacturer and ask Him to restore us back to our original God-like settings. When you take a computer into a specialist, they don't mask over the virus; they remove it from the system. God wants to give you a complete reset of your toxic emotions, so they are gone out of your life forever.

Does that seem impossible?

The ultimate reset is when you accept Christ as your Savior. In that moment, God totally restores you to your original settings and wipes away your old life as if it never happened. You no longer have your former settings, and you've been given back the original "Garden of Eden" emotions of perfect union and communion with God.

In that moment of spiritual reset, all the old bugs and viruses of your past are removed, and you receive a spotless spirit. No matter what you've done in the past, this makes you a new creation, and your spirit becomes one hundred percent holy, righteous, perfect, without sin, and pleasing to God. When God looks at you, he no longer sees your mistakes, but he sees Christ in you, making you perfect and in His image.

If you have never been saved or had that spiritual reset, emotional freedom is impossible. It is a gift of grace for the believer. You can receive that salvation right now if you haven't already. Say this Prayer:

God, I thank you for forgiving me of all my sins. I confess with my mouth that Jesus is Lord and that you raised Him from the dead. I invite Him into my heart to become my Lord and Savior. In Jesus's Name. Amen.

If you openly declare that Jesus is Lord and believe in your heart that God raised Him from the dead, you will be saved. That is the promise of the Bible. That's what makes emotional freedom possible. For it is by believing in your heart that you are made right with God, and it is by openly declaring your faith that you are saved. The end result is a brand-new life that can only come from the Creator.

The Bible says that you are born again when you accept Christ as your Savior. Those words are reset words. Born again means the old things are passed away, and all things are new. Only God can do such a transformation, and He wants to do it for everyone who believes in His Son.

For those of you reading this who are already saved, Jesus wants to give you an abundant life. However, you have to receive that in the same way you receive salvation. It doesn't just happen automatically. Even though God has restored you back to the way things were in the Garden of Eden in your spirit, not everything is exactly the same. Adam and Eve had no knowledge of good and evil and weren't corrupted by sin. Once they sinned, they had the knowledge of evil, and their emotions were corrupted. You have that knowledge of evil as well, so you must live with the consequences and feel the pain of knowing evil. So, how can your emotions be restored to the original settings while there are still troubles that can corrupt your emotions?

Look at what happened to the Apostle Paul. Paul said that he was the "chief among sinners." And He was. He went about capturing and murdering Christians. He consented to the stoning of Stephen, one of the great men of God, who helped start the early church. But Paul had a salvation experience on the road to Damascus, and his life was transformed. That's why he could write with such authority.

In Second Corinthians 7:2, Paul made this statement: "I have wronged no one." On the surface, that would sound like a lie. He did wrong Stephen when he consented to his stoning. How is it that Paul could have a clear conscience? It's because of the system reset. He was born again. He became a new creation. The old things have passed away. They were no more.

Only God can do such a transformation. God is the one who is merciful. All your sins and lawless deeds were forgotten. Paul murdered Christians. That was forgotten, thanks to God's mercy. God does the same thing for you that He did for Paul. All your sins are forgotten. They are no more. He has done a total factory reset of your life and has restored you to the original factory settings.

Notice what else Paul also said later in that chapter: "I am filled with comfort. I am exceedingly joyful in our tribulation."

Not only did Paul experience a spiritual reset; he received a reset of his emotions. In this new state of mind, he was filled with comfort. He was "exceedingly" joyful when troubles came.

How is that possible and is it possible for you?

You Are a Three-Part Being

God is a three part being—Father, Son, and Holy Spirit—and we're made in God's image. According to the Bible, you have a spirit, soul, and body. Your spirit is eternal and was made alive in Christ at salvation. Your soul is your mind, will, and emotions. Your body is your flesh which will pass away when you die.

If you are a Christian, then your spirit has been made perfect through Christ. When you were born-again at salvation, the Spirit of God came to live in you and set you free from sin. The above verse says God is making you holy in every way. He does that through the leading of His Spirit within you. To be whole and blameless means you have surrendered your soul (mind, will, and emotions) to His greater purposes and allowed Him to rule and reign in your heart.

Your spirit, through Christ living in you, is perfect. Your mind and emotions, however, are not perfect. They must be transformed over time. That's called sanctification. Your feelings originate in your soul. They must be changed over time by your spirit and brought into the control of your spirit. That's why you're born again and can still sin, and you still sometimes respond with negative toxic emotions.

There's a division between your spirit and your soul that must be broken down to have abundant life. You must get the truth that now resides in your spirit to take over the emotions in your soul. This comes by reading, memorizing, meditating on, and following the truth of God's Word and letting God break down that division.

Breaking Down the Division Between Your Spirit and Soul

For the word of God is living and powerful, and sharper than any two-edged sword, piercing even to the division of soul and spirit, and of joints and marrow, and is a discerner of the thoughts and intents of the heart. (Hebrews 4:12 NKJV)

There is a division between your soul and your spirit. You have everything you need in your spirit to live an abundant life. Your spirit never sins and always responds with the proper emotions to every circumstance including troubles. In your spirit, you have love, joy, peace, patience, kindness, goodness, faith, gentleness, and self-control. These are called the fruit of the Spirit (Galatians 5:22). The problem is that what is in your spirit is not always manifested in your flesh. Your goal should be to silence your flesh and be led by the Spirit. But all too often, this is not the case.

Instead of love, which is a fruit of the spirit, you may feel hatred, resentment, and bitterness in your heart. Instead of joy, you may feel sadness and depression. Peace may be overwhelmed by anxiety. Patience may give way to frustration. Instead of kindness, you can be mean. Rather than respond in goodness, you may have evil thoughts and intentions. Faith is often overcome by fear. Instead of gentleness, you can be harsh and unforgiving, or proud and haughty. Self-control can be ignored as you become obsessed and walk in the lust of the flesh, indulging in sinful and addictive behaviors that are destructive. That's the division between the soul and the spirit. That's the difference between walking in the flesh and walking in the Spirit.

Hebrews 4:12 says the Word of God breaks down (pierces) that division. In other words, the Word of God breaks down the wall that keeps the Spirit and the fruit of the Spirit from flowing through to your flesh. A dam controls the flow of water to a river or a lake. The dam is small compared to the size of the lake, but it can easily control the water if it is designed properly. Imagine a huge dam in your heart that blocks the flow of the Spirit to your heart. The dam in your heart is controlling the power of the Holy Spirit from manifesting in your life. That's why you continually feel negative emotions even though the Holy Spirit is living inside of you.

> So I say, let the Holy Spirit guide your lives. Then you won't be doing what your sinful nature craves. The sinful nature wants to do evil, which is just the opposite of what the Spirit wants. And the Spirit gives us desires that are the opposite of what the sinful nature desires. These two forces are constantly fighting each other, so you are not free to carry out your good intentions. But when you are directed by the Spirit, you are not under obligation to the law of Moses. (Galatians 5:16-18)

This verse describes very clearly the battle happening inside every believer. Your spirit wants to do the right thing. Your flesh is the opposite and desires sin. They fight against each other. When you give in to the flesh, you allow sin into your life and your emotions are affected.

This verse describes what happens to you when you sin and identifies the problem:

> When you follow the desires of your sinful nature, the results are very clear: sexual immorality, impurity, lustful pleasures, idolatry, sorcery, hostility, quarreling, jealousy, outbursts of anger, selfish ambition, dissension, division, envy, drunkenness, wild parties, and other sins like these. (Galatians 5:19-21)

This verse describes the solution:

Those who belong to Christ Jesus have nailed the passions and desires of their sinful nature to his cross and crucified them there. Since we are living by the Spirit, let us follow the Spirit's leading in every part of our lives. Let us not become conceited, or provoke one another, or be jealous of one another. (Galatians 5:24-26)

The first verse describes many negative emotions. It says when you're following the desires of your sinful nature, you'll have outbursts of anger, lusts, jealousy, envy, divisions, and other similar negative and toxic emotions. When the Holy Spirit is in control of those who belong to Christ and have nailed the passions and sinful desires to the cross, with the fruit of the Spirit dominant in their lives they are able to overcome those negative emotions and are free to carry out God's will for their lives.

The verse says to follow the Spirit's leading in every part of your life, including your spirit, soul, and body. You "feel free" by the power of the Spirit of the Lord living inside you. Have you ever had a kink in your water hose, and the water wouldn't flow out? Most Christians live with kinks in the connection between their spirit and their soul. I want to help you clear that connection so the fruit of the Spirit will flow freely between your spirit and your soul, and your flesh will be transformed by the power of God.

Let God Purify Your Conscience

Just think how much more the blood of Christ will purify our
consciences from sinful deeds so that we can worship the living God.
For by the power of the eternal Spirit, Christ offered himself
to God as a perfect sacrifice for our sins.
(Hebrews 9:14)

Your conscience is filled with the memory of your past sins and the
knowledge of the evil of those sins. For many people, the memory of
those sins keeps them bound to shame, depression, guilt, and a sense
of feeling worthless. The blood of Christ, however, was shed to
cleanse you of your sins and purify your conscience. You can stand
before God whole, perfect and in the right relationship between
God and self, knowing Christ has set you free from the penalty or
curse of that sin.

The word *purify* means to sanitize or disinfect. It's like cleaning
your kitchen. You sanitize your counter to remove all the unwanted
germs and bacteria that can make you sick. God wants to completely
sanitize your conscience from your past sins, so it doesn't make you
emotionally sick.

The first step to emotional freedom is to accept God's forgiveness
and let Him clean your soul. The second step in the process of emotional freedom is to forgive others.

Total, Complete, Unconditional Forgiveness

And be kind to one another, tenderhearted, forgiving one another,
even as God in Christ forgave you.
(Ephesians 4:32 NKJV)

Have you ever tasted the individual ingredients of a chocolate cake?
Ingredients like cocoa and baking soda are bitter and hard to taste

by themselves. However, when they're put into the hands of a master baker, they can be blended to produce a delicious cake that's very enjoyable. When sugar is added to practically anything, it enhances the taste. You can add sugar to something sour, and it'll become sweet. This is a phenomenon in creation. God has created many things to be enhanced when they're combined with other things.

The two elements of table salt are sodium and chlorine. They're both highly deadly if ingested on their own. When combined, they're perfectly healthy to consume. The physical properties of each negate the deadly properties of the other.

Hydrogen is a highly flammable gas. So is oxygen. Hydrogen and oxygen on their own are extremely combustible and can cause deadly and catastrophic explosions and fires. Together, however, they form water. Water is used to put out fires! It's amazing how God uses opposite things to minimize the dangerous properties of the other.

The emotional roots of bitterness, anger, resentment, and unforgiveness are dangerous to your emotional well-being. Life can be painful. People can hurt you. The raw emotions of rejection, abandonment, abuse, and betrayal can bring authentic pain when they happen. Most emotional roots are caused by something someone else has done to you. God knew we would hurt each other, so he developed a way in which to be healed immediately from those hurts. It's called forgiveness.

When forgiveness is applied to bitterness, it takes away all its power to hurt you and becomes part of the abundant blessings of God. Forgiveness is like sugar mixed with cocoa. It produces something pleasing. When the fruit of the Spirit is applied to all your negative emotions, the dangerous emotions lose all their power. You can literally remove all past hurts and emotional roots by forgiveness to the point that they are no longer recognizable inside you. It's a powerful tool of restoration and healing.

Forgiveness is the key to freedom and an emotional reset. Christ eliminated all the power of your sins to produce death in you in one moment on the cross. God's forgiveness totally transformed your destiny.

God's forgiveness changes sins that are red and turns them white. White is symbolic of cleanliness. Red stains clothes. In fact, I'm told by my wife that red stains are the hardest to get out of clothes. Sin stains our soul like red stains a piece of cloth. God adds forgiveness to the sins, and we become perfectly clean and without spot or blemish (Ephesians 5:27). That's not unlike a soiled piece of clothing that's perfectly clean after it's been washed. Forgiveness is the powerful tool God uses to transform your soul and cleanse you of all your sins.

God's forgiveness cleanses *all* your unrighteousness. Forgiveness has that much power. It can take every act of unrighteousness that occurs through an entire lifetime and remove the stain of that unrighteousness and make you totally and completely righteous before God. Aren't you glad God removes "all" of your sins and cleanses you from all unrighteousness?

Forgive One Another as God has Forgiven You

The motivation for forgiving others is that God has forgiven you. You're to forgive as the Lord has forgiven you. The same power of forgiveness that cleanses you from your sins can remove the stain that other's sins have caused in your life. Answer this question: Do you want partial forgiveness from God, or do you want God to forgive you of all your faults and offenses?

The Bible says several times to make allowances for each other's faults. In other words, go ahead and accept the fact that other people will offend you. The Greek word for *offend* means to cause to stumble. It's where we get our word "scandalize" which means to shock or horrify. Generally, when we think of someone offending us, we think of it as something they've done to hurt us. It actually means they've done something to make us offended or indignant about their actions.

Someone offending us is actually an opportunity for us to stumble if we don't forgive them. That offense can turn into unforgiveness, which will turn into a root of bitterness, which opens the door to the enemy.

Forgiveness Must be Unconditional

I recently read excerpts from a best-selling book that was a personal memoir. The author shared her "hellish nightmare" upon discovering her husband's affair. She described the emotional pain she felt for years at his betrayal. The book is about forgiveness and eventually she got there. But how much unnecessary pain did she endure by not getting there right away?

Far too many times, I've heard or read statements like these:

"You've got a long road ahead of you."

"You never really get over the grief of a loss."

"Things are hard. This pain will never completely go away."

At the risk of sounding judgmental, I totally reject those thoughts. I don't deny that most people struggle with the pain of emotions for years when they experience deep emotional traumas. They are called wounds. What I do reject is the notion that the pain from wounds have to continue on indefinitely.

Forgiveness is the ultimate emotional reset for wounds. It allows you to resolve an issue and offense with another person immediately and cleanses your conscience and allows you the emotional freedom to move on. People will hurt you. There will be offenses. You will hurt others. That's part of this fallen world. That's why Jesus died so we could have an emotional reset every time an offense occurs.

The emotional reset comes in the form of forgiveness. It is the quick way to resolve offenses. Really, it's the *only* way. When someone offends you, it is nearly impossible to get over the offense without forgiveness.

How are we to forgive? The way God forgives us. His forgiveness is unconditional, and He doesn't hold the sin against us anymore. That's what He expects of us. In fact, how arrogant and selfish would it be of us to receive God's unconditional forgiveness for everything, but not grant that same forgiveness to others?

The discretion of a man makes him slow to anger, And his glory is to overlook a transgression. (Proverbs 19:11 NKJV)

Your glory is to overlook a transgression. That's called grace. Unmerited favor. It is actually your glory. You are never more like God than when you love and forgive transgression.

What if the other person doesn't deserve it? We don't deserve grace either. That's why it is called unmerited favor. When you overlook a transgression, even something as devastating emotionally as adultery, the glory of the Lord is manifesting inside of you. That doesn't mean you have to stay married to the person. It doesn't mean you have to continue to be abused by someone.

Forgiveness is for your benefit, not theirs. It is your path to feeling free.

PART TWO

WHAT EMOTIONAL FREEDOM FEELS LIKE

"In order to move on, you must understand why you felt what you did, and why you no longer need to feel it."
Mitch Albom

FROM THE AUTHOR

In this second part of the book, I want to show you the difference between the fruit of the Spirit and the lust of the flesh and how they are contrary to each other. You will see that many feelings are the direct opposite of the fruit of the Spirit and what God intended for you in the area of emotions.

When people are suffering from heartache and deep hurts, they often cry out to God for help. The problem is that they are asking God for something He has already given to them. If I gave my son a new car for his birthday, how foolish would it be for him to keep asking me to buy him a car? The same thing is true when we ask God for peace or joy. He's already given it to us through the person of the Holy Spirit who dwells inside of us.

Everything you need for emotional freedom is right inside of you in the form of the fruit of the Spirit. All you have to do is access it. If my son asked me to buy him a car, I'd tell him to go in the driveway and drive the one he already has. If we ask God for peace, if He wasn't so merciful, I'm sure He would be thinking, "I've already given you peace. Just receive it."

The problem is that Satan has counterfeited all of the fruit of the Spirit in the form of negative emotions. The fruit of the Spirit are love, joy, peace, patience, kindness, goodness, faithfulness, gentleness, and self-control.[1]

Look out how the enemy has counterfeited each of these with negative emotions:

Love-Lust

Joy-Depression, Sorrow

Peace-Anxiety

Patience-Discontent

Kindness-Anger

Goodness-Shame

Faithfulness-Fear

Gentleness-Pride

Self-Control-Addictions

As you can see, the toxic emotions on the right are the direct opposite of what God intended for you to feel when He gave you emotions.

So, what does "feeling free" feel like? It feels like walking in the spirit and not in the flesh. It is the manifestation of the fruit into your everyday life. Over the next few chapters, I'm going to contrast the two and show you how the feelings of the flesh are counterfeit and not even real and then how to access God's emotional provisions for you through the fruit of the Spirit.

Thank you for letting me take you on this journey. I pray that God will use it to bring real and lasting freedom to your soul.

~Terry Toler

8

Freedom from Lust

Love is the root of all that's good. God is love, and anyone who doesn't love doesn't know God according to the Bible. First Corinthians 13 says love is the greatest when compared to faith and hope and everything else for that matter. Love can heal the broken hearted, set captives free, and can be the most fulfilling of all characteristics of God. However, when love is counterfeited, it is in the form of lust. Lust is a toxic emotion rather than a spiritual attribute of God and it gets twisted, manipulated, and dangerous.

In reality, lust is not even an emotion. It's a desire that is birthed in sin. The Greek word for *lust* is a desire for evil. It is literally a craving for something that is wrong. To the person tempted by lust, it seems like a feeling. The urge can "feel" overwhelming. Euphoric even. Overwhelming joy and happiness can enhance the feelings of the lust. What most don't realize is that the feelings are counterfeit and not real. They feel real but aren't based in reality. They feel true but aren't based upon the truth.

Another definition of *feeling* is to reach out and touch. It can mean to grip or feel something with your hand or another part of your body. That is what lust is. It's a temptation. A desire inside you contrary to the Word of God which is prompting you to desire and/ or reach out and touch something that is not of God and is destructive for you.

Not unlike when Adam and Eve ate from the tree of the knowledge of good and evil. The Bible says that the fruit looked "pleasing" to them.[3] The desire to eat from the tree became so overwhelming, especially when they felt it with their hands. Once they saw that they didn't die from touching it, they took it a step further and ate it.

Sin is birthed from lust or wrong desires which come out of the heart. When desire is conceived inside a person, he is enticed by his willingness to act upon that desire. That lust could be anything contrary to God's Word. It could be another person you want to touch in an immoral relationship. It could be a desire to buy something you can't afford. It can even be something you want to eat or drink that tastes good in the moment but will cause health problems later on. Maybe even as soon as tonight in the form of a stomach ache or acid reflux, or perhaps in the morning in the form of a hangover.

Lust gives birth to sin and when it is acted upon (felt or touched), it brings forth death. Somewhere in that process are feelings. The act of sin may bring temporary happiness. Even a sense of euphoria, usually followed by guilt. Perhaps even shame and condemnation. While feelings are so intertwined in lust, it's hard to differentiate between the two. The lust itself is not an emotion even though it feels like it. It's the counterfeit to the first fruit of the Spirit and the greatest of them all: Love.

True love isn't even an emotion. It's not a feeling; it's a choice. Most people don't fully understand love and confuse love and lust all the time. That feeling of lust is not true love. In fact, it's impossible to love apart from God. Here's what the Bible says:

> Dear friends, let us love one another for love comes from God. Everyone who loves has been born of God and knows God. Whoever does not love does not know God, because God is love. (1 John 4:7-8 NIV)

For all that is in the world—the lust of the flesh, the lust of the eyes, and the pride of life—is not of the Father but is of the world. (1 John 2:16 NKJV)

Let's consider these verses together. The first verse says that God is love and love comes from God. The second verse says that the lust of the flesh, the lust of the eyes, and the pride of life are not from God but are from the world. Only one conclusion can be drawn from these verses: Any feelings of love that are not from God are not really love.

Feelings that come from immoral and adulterous relationships are not love. They may feel like love, but they are really lust. Don't let yourself be deceived. Real love comes from God. Any relationship that is contrary to the will of God for your life cannot be love because it is conceived from lust and the desire leads to sin.

A caller on one of my talk shows asked, "Should I marry my boyfriend, even though we would be unequally yoked?" Second Corinthians 6:14 clearly says not to be unequally yoked with unbelievers. In other words, don't marry an unbeliever. Don't even date an unbeliever because you can't mix light with darkness. It will almost always end in disaster. The way she worded the question made it obvious she already knew the answer; she just didn't want to accept it.

After I quoted for her the verse about being unequally yoked, she started crying and said, "But I love him."

I said to her, "No you don't. It's impossible."

That made her mad. "How dare you say that I don't love him?"

I quoted the verse about love coming from God. Then I asked her, "Why would God command you in His Word to not marry an unbeliever, but at the same time give you love for an unbeliever?"

He wouldn't. That's the point. What she was feeling was lust of the flesh. That lust will turn to an action, which will lead to sin and ultimately death. I have no idea what happened with that woman, but if she continued on that path, I almost guarantee she regretted it at some point. If I could talk to her now and she were completely honest, she'd probably say that the pain of continuing the relationship and the way it ended was much worse than just breaking it off when she had the chance.

The truth is that authentic love can only be a reality and good for you when rooted in God. If it violates God's Word, it can't be love. It can be the human emotion of liking someone or perhaps lusting for them, but to be true love it must be pure and from God. Therefore, it's impossible for you to truly be in love with an unbeliever as God wouldn't authorize an unequal yoke.

All sexual impurity and immorality are works of the flesh that lead to bondage. It's a misstatement of fact for someone to say they are in love with someone who they are in an immoral, homosexual, or adulterous relationship with. It's not love; it's a work of the flesh. It's a counterfeit emotion meant to mask itself as real love.

Does that mean that an unbeliever is incapable of love? Not at all. God can give love to anyone when it is the right relationship. The worst gangster in the mafia can love his mother. He can even love his wife because it is in the realm of marriage. However, he can't love his mistress. God would never give him love for her.

You can love your neighbor as yourself because God has given everyone the ability to love their neighbor. However, in a romantic relationship, any real love can only come from God, and God desires for that to be exclusive and in the context of marriage between a man and a woman.

Lustful Feelings are Unnaturally Enhanced by the Enemy

In the same way the men also abandoned natural relations with
women and were **inflamed** with lust for one another.
(Romans 1:27 NIV Emphasis added)

The Bible says that lust can be inflamed. The definition of *inflamed* is
provoked or stirred. This suggests an outside stimulus. A fire is inflamed when it's stirred with a poker stick. The flames intensify and
grow stronger.

Another definition of *inflamed* is to incite. I would suggest to you
that the lusts of the flesh are enhanced, stirred up, and inflamed by
the enemy to make the desires seem stronger than they actually are.

Remember, God intended for emotions to be based on reality.
Those counterfeit feelings of love that aren't from God are destructive for you, and they're anchored in your human desires. So many
Christians enter into relationships that aren't from God because
they "feel" like they're in love. Then they make lifetime decisions
based on something that's not real and marry the wrong person. It
almost always ends in disaster. When the feelings leave, they believe
they're not in love with the person anymore, so they want out of the
relationship.

That's the deception in adultery. Many Christians enter into
adulterous relationships because the passion and romance feels like
love. But love is not a feeling. That means what they are experiencing is lust, not love. It may look like love, feel like love, and even
take on the same characteristics of love, but it isn't love. In fact, it's
another form of twisted bondage and deception. The lust of the
flesh is wrong, and Satan even enhances (inflames) the emotional
feelings or attraction to make you think they are real and better
than they actually are.

My wife and I have counseled many people over the years who've had affairs. They always describe the feelings as intense and so different than the feelings they have for their partner. They explain the powerful emotions or physical attraction the adulterous partner provides, and they think it's authentic. They may even call it love. But those feelings are twisted emotions sent by the enemy, no different than the ones Adam and Eve felt when they were enticed to eat from the fruit found on the tree of good and evil.

Why can such immoral feelings be so intense and seem so right? Because the enemy is the master of deception and lies. He intensifies the feelings, so you want to do them, and he doesn't tell you the pain that is just around the corner when he takes those feelings away.

The lustful feelings are also intensified by other emotions. Fear and anxiety that come from the risk of carrying on a secret affair add to the inflamed emotions. At some point, they come to a crashing halt and are replaced with guilt, shame, and condemnation when the secret relationship is discovered.

Once the affair is in the open, and Satan has destroyed the marriage, the intense feelings go away. That's why marriages that start from an adulterous relationship almost always end in divorce. The percentage is around ninety-seven percent. The couple thinks what they're feeling is love, so they leave their spouse for what feels good and fills an emotional need. The truth is that they've hardened their hearts from hearing God's voice and their twisted lust and craving for selfish desires entangles them in a web of deception.

Here's how the enemy works. As long as the sex is wrong and outside of marriage, it feels erotic, unbelievable, uncontrollable, and even spiritual. But what most don't realize is that those emotions aren't love. They aren't from God. He would never violate his covenant and never lead us into sin. Once a person leaves his or her spouse and marries the adulterous partner, they begin to think they're legally out of the woods of immorality. That's when the enemy exits the scene, removes the erotic emotions, and leaves the adulterous couple with nothing more than another discontented relationship. Most couples who started from an adulterous affair, eventually relate to us in counseling that the second marriage is worse than the first.

Why is that? The enhancement is gone. The sexual marriage act is no longer wrong. Consequently, sex is no longer mysterious and exciting. The couple thinks they aren't in love anymore, and they get a divorce or commit adultery again with someone else so they can get those feelings back. And Satan is working behind the scenes to make sure they have all the feelings he wants them to have. Before, he was trying to keep the adulterous couple together; once they're married, he's trying to tear them apart.

You can only find true love when it's given to you by God. Any relationship you enter into that isn't of God or violates his Word isn't true love, no matter how strong the feelings. How do you get over the feelings then?

If you're feeling hurt over what you think is a lost love from your past, ask yourself if that relationship was from God. If it wasn't, then it wasn't true love, and you can ask God for freedom from the spiritual yoke of bondage it created. If you've lost what was a true love, that doesn't mean you can never find love again. You just must seek out the true love that only God can give. If you're in an immoral relationship, end it immediately, receive God's forgiveness, and let Him give you peace to overcome the guilt and the pain of the broken relationship.

If it's impossible to unscramble the eggs and the damage is already done, that doesn't mean you can never find true love again. God can redeem any situation even if you've missed the mark. What it does mean is that you can only find true love when it is given to you by God. Any relationship that you enter into that is not of God is not true love no matter how strong the feelings. Because God is a God of redemption, you can find true love from God again but only if you reject the lust of the flesh and seek the "true love of your life" based on God's plan for your life.

9

Freedom from Depression

My wife, Donna, is an accomplished flutist. She carries her flute in a backpack along with a stand, supplies, and her music folder. Fully loaded, the backpack weighs between twelve to fifteen pounds. Easily manageable for her, but it can get heavy if she has to carry it for a long distance. Imagine if she had to carry that backpack around every day, twenty-four hours a day and was never able to set it down. How manageable would it be if she had to sleep with it, cook with it, drive with it, and never get any relief from it? Within a short period of time, the flute, which brings her tremendous joy, would become a heavy burden.

Sins is called weights in the Bible. The race of life set before us requires endurance and weights make running the race harder. I've already talked about how hard life can be with the troubles everyone must face. Past hurts and future worries are like weights. They lead to toxic emotions like depression and sorrow. The race is made more difficult when those emotions are weighing us down.

Jesus said He would provide rest and an easier burden for those who are weary and are weighed down and heavy laden. This is a supernatural act of grace for the believer to relieve him of his sorrows and depression.

> Surely, he hath borne our griefs, and carried our sorrows.
> (Isaiah 53:4 KJV)

The *He* in this passage is Jesus. He carried your sorrows. What does that mean?

Over the past few years, my wife and I have done a lot of traveling. When we have a trip scheduled, my wife starts packing weeks in advance. I have jokingly said to her that it seems like she enjoys the packing as much as she enjoys the actual trip. My wife is a professional packer. She has it down to a science. We decided a long time ago that we were going to pack light and we didn't want to check any bags, which makes her job harder.

Several years ago, we went to Italy and Israel for three weeks, and she packed everything she needed into one small suitcase and a backpack. It's amazing how proficient she is at making sure she has everything she needs and yet economizes so we don't have to check any bags.

Even with the small suitcase and backpack, the luggage can be heavy in certain situations. If we have to climb stairs or load the bags into the rental car van or walk a distance to our hotel, even a small suitcase can be heavy for her. Many times, I will carry my bags and her suitcase. I don't mind, and it makes things easier for her and scores me some "gentleman" points.

The above verse says that Jesus bore our sorrows. Surely, it says He bore them. The word "surely" is there for emphasis. So that we know it is definitive. We learned in an earlier chapter that the definition of "bore" means to carry. Donna's bags are a picture of what Christ did when He bore our sins, admittedly, on a much smaller scale. Nevertheless, when I take Donna's suitcase from her, I am taking it upon myself to carry it, and she is free from the burden. In a similar, but much more profound way, Christ took our sins, carried them Himself, and freed us from the burden of those sins.

It is a free gift. A porter will carry your bags if you pay him. I carry Donna's bags for free because I love her. Jesus carries our pain and suffering for free because He loves us!

What to Do When Sorrow Seems Overwhelming

The book of Lamentations is about a man struggling with his emotions. Written by the prophet, Jeremiah, he prophesied the destruction of Jerusalem and it came to pass. The entire book is about his grief over Babylon invading Jerusalem and destroying the entire city.

The word *lamentation* means the passionate expression of grief or sorrow. Lamentations says that thousands of young men and women were killed and many more were taken into slavery. Jeremiah lamented, or remembered in grief, how they used to eat the best delicacies and wore the finest clothes, but now they were all destitute, living on the streets, begging for bread, racked with hunger, and wasting away from a lack of food. He was distraught over the circumstances. Lamentations is a raw reflection of Jeremiah's toxic emotions and cry of desperation.

And it was all preventable. Jeremiah had tried for forty years to get the people of Israel to repent. If they had repented, they would have spared themselves that suffering. He could do nothing about it at that point, so he had given up hope. Jeremiah had every reason to grieve. He was at the lowest point in his life.

And you will be sorrowful, but your sorrow will be turned into joy.
(John 16:20 NKJV)

Those were Jesus's words. He said we would have sorrow. Then He gave us an amazing promise, "Your sorrow will be turned into joy." This is a supernatural occurrence. I like to give you definitions of words. The Greek word for *turned* means a dynamic change of direction or a circular reversal. One minute you are feeling sorrow; the next minute you are feeling joy.

Weeping may endure for a night, But joy comes in the morning.
(Psalm 30:5 NKJV)

Even sorrow is supposed to be temporary. Depression is supposed
to last through the night, but in the morning things should change.
There can be a dramatic turn of events at sunlight. It doesn't mean
the circumstances will change, but how they affect your emotions
will change. It can only happen if you let Jesus turn your sorrow to
joy.

Seem impossible?

Do you remember the story of Shadrach, Meshach, and Abednego? They lived during the same time as Jeremiah. They were young
men who were taken as slaves to Babylon to live under the tyranni-
cal rule of King Nebuchadnezzar. Jeremiah was left in Jerusalem to
suffer with the rest of the people. Shadrach, Meshach, and Abednego had it just as bad. They were young, strong, and vibrant men
who were taken to Babylon as slaves and put in the king's army.

King Nebuchadnezzar built a statue and ordered every person to
bow down before his image. Shadrach, Meshach, and Abednego refused to worship the statue. The king flew into a rage and told them
that if they refused, he would have them thrown into a blazing furnace. In Daniel chapter three, the three men said that God would
save them and, even if He didn't, they still wouldn't bow down and
worship the statue of the king.

How did they handle their emotions differently than Jeremiah?
Jeremiah was moaning and groaning and complaining about his situation and how God had abandoned them. The three boys responded to their hardship with faith. They trusted God. They
weren't crying or complaining or blaming God. In fact, they rose up
in defiance of the king.

King Nebuchadnezzar followed through with his threats and threw them into the furnace. They did not cower in fear. They defied the King! "We will never bow down. God will deliver us," were their mighty words of faith. Can you hear the determination in their voices? Can you see their unwillingness to let the sorrow overcome them? As I mentioned earlier, it didn't mean that their circumstances changed. They were facing what appeared to be certain death. But their circumstances didn't determine their mood. They refused to be sorrowful or to mourn or be depressed.

Because of their faith they were rescued from the fiery furnace.

God's Mercies are New Every Morning

How can you feel joy in the morning when the day before brought you great heartache and perhaps even tragedy? It's because of God's mercies. You are not expected to turn your sorrow into joy with your own strength. That's not humanly possible. Only the mercy of God allows such a transformation of emotions. Even Jeremiah eventually came to that understanding:

> My soul is downcast within me. Yet this I call to mind and therefore I have hope: Because of the Lord's great love we are not consumed, for his compassions never fail. They are new every morning; great is your faithfulness.
> (Lamentations 3:20-23 NIV)

> For he does not willingly bring affliction or grief to anyone.
> (Lamentations 3:33 NIV)

Jeremiah said that he called new thoughts to his mind. Remember how I said in previous chapters that feelings come from thoughts. Transformation comes through the renewing of your mind and changing your thoughts. Jeremiah's emotions were changed when his thoughts changed. His soul was downcast. Yet, a new thought came to his mind and he had hope.

When he remembered those new thoughts, everything changed, and he felt hope again. He called to mind that God was compassionate and faithful. He also remembered that his belief that God caused his afflictions was not correct. Throughout the first two chapters of Lamentations, Jeremiah blamed God for their suffering. In this chapter, he suddenly remembered that God does not willingly bring affliction or grief to anyone!

Remember, just because you believe something doesn't make it true.

Jeremiah believed God had caused his afflictions. That was not true, and he was depressed because he believed the lies. The world tells you to validate your feelings, acknowledge them as your truth, and then live out the feelings with confidence in who you are. Do you see how dangerous this really is? If you are like most people, feelings change. To validate or follow your feelings could mean that you are following a lie.

Jeremiah invalidated his feelings. He awakened to the truth and began to make decisions according to God's promises. In Lamentations 3:18, Jeremiah lamented that his "hope was gone." In Lamentations 3:21, he invalidated that feeling and said "therefore, I have hope."

What a complete transformation and renewing of his mind! What if he had continued to believe that he had no hope? He would have continued to be depressed. As soon as he remembered God's faithfulness and compassion, he realized that he did have hope, and his feelings changed. His circumstances didn't change; his thoughts about them changed and so did his feelings.

Yet, a Powerful Three-Letter Word

Remember the word *yet*. Jeremiah used it to transition his thoughts. Verse twenty says he was downcast. Verse twenty-one starts with Jeremiah saying "yet." That was the transition from negative feelings and wrong believing to remembering the truth. What did Jeremiah say in the transition? "Yet, this I call to mind."

In other words, he all of a sudden remembered something important, awakened to the truth, and began to move in a new direction. This is the essence of what it means to repent. You come to your senses and realize, "Wait, what I'm doing isn't right. I need to re-think my life and head in a different direction." Likewise, that's how you get over your negative emotions. You repent. You think differently. You do an about-face.

No matter how long it takes, you decide to get to "yet" as quickly as possible and allow it to become the roadblock set against the enemy's plan to destroy your life. Every time you feel a negative emotion, say the word "yet" and then add something from God's Word to it.

The doctor told me I have cancer, **yet**, by His stripes I am healed (1 Peter 2:24). We are in a desperate financial situation, **yet**, God said he would supply all my needs according to his riches in glory (Philippians 4:19). My husband died, **yet**, I have the hope that he is with the Lord (1 Thessalonians 4:13). I just lost my job, **yet**, God said he causes all things to work together for my good (Romans 8:28).

That's renewing your mind by repentance through the Word of God. Remember, repentance is changing your mind. What are you changing your mind to? You're changing your mind to God's way of thinking from his Word. That is renewing your mind. That's the total opposite to how the world tells you to handle feelings.

113

Once your mind is renewed and you bring your emotions under control, then your actions will change. That doesn't necessarily mean your circumstances will change but now you have the strength to endure them without sinking into depression.

You Can Have Joy Even in Loss

When they reached the threshing floor of Atad, near the Jordan, they lamented loudly and bitterly; and there Joseph observed **a seven-day period of mourning** for his father.
(Genesis 50:10 NIV Emphasis added).

Joseph mourned the loss of his father. It says they lamented loudly and bitterly. Those are strong emotions. Over the years, I've seen tremendous grief in those who have suffered any number of losses. The death of a parent, child, spouse, grandparent, friend, or even the loss of a pet can evoke tremendous grief.

In the Old Testament, God set a specific time period for mourning. Seven days. By the instruction of the law and by Jewish culture, seven days was the allotted time for grieving, and after that they were to return to their normal lives. In the case of Moses, thirty days of grieving was allowed after his death because of his status.

Even then, God did not want them to grieve indefinitely. Grief needed to be for a specific time frame so that the grief did not turn into depression. Notice what happened earlier in Genesis when Jacob thought his son, Joseph, was dead:

Then Jacob tore his clothes and dressed himself in burlap. He mourned deeply for his son for a long time. His family all tried to comfort him, but he refused to be comforted. "I will go to my grave mourning for my son," he would say, and then he would weep.
(Genesis 37:34-35)

Jacob refused to be comforted. He allowed his grief to go on indefinitely beyond the seven days. Consequently, he sunk into depression and wept constantly. It's interesting to note that Joseph wasn't actually dead. Joseph's brothers were jealous and sold him into slavery and pretended he had died. Jacob didn't know Joseph was still alive, so he mourned deeply and for a long period of time. He refused to be comforted by anyone and refused to follow the instructions to only mourn for a determined period of time.

Jacob was grieving over a lie. His son was actually alive, and Jacob would see him again. He still might've grieved over his son being in slavery, but it wouldn't have been as traumatic. Many of our griefs aren't based on reality. Even if they're based on real facts, there is supposed to be a period of time when our sorrows are over. Even in the most traumatic times, such as losing a loved one, the sorrows are supposed to last for a limited time, and your weeping is supposed to turn to laughter and your mourning, into dancing.

However, you can refuse to be comforted. You can be like Jacob and speak the words that you're going to grieve for the rest of your life. When you allow yourself to feel sorrow for longer than a short period of time, it will turn into the toxic emotion of depression and eventually sickness and disease.

Jacob lived under the old covenant and was given seven days to grieve. Look at what Paul said about grief in the new covenant after the death of Christ:

And now, dear brothers and sisters, we want you to know what will
happen to the believers who have died so you will not grieve like
people who have no hope. For since we believe that Jesus died and
was raised to life again, we also believe that when Jesus returns, God
will bring back with him the believers who have died.
(1 Thessalonians 4: 13-14)

Paul said you don't have to grieve at all! The world grieves because they have no hope. We have the hope that we'll see our loved one again. Paul said absent from the body means we are present with the Lord. [13] Therefore, if you believe that fact, then there's no reason to grieve. In reality, there are many reasons to rejoice. In the Old Testament, the mourning lasted for seven days. In the new covenant, your mourning should turn to joy immediately.

This is true for every sorrow. If Christ has freed you from every sorrow, you only have to feel the sorrow as long as it takes you to remember that Christ has carried it. As soon as you remember the provision of Christ on the cross, you should feel immediate joy, and the sadness will go away.

Your suffering is only supposed to be short-term, and God Himself will restore you and make you strong, firm, and steadfast. While you may have troubles that create suffering and sorrows, they're supposed to be temporary. The definition of *steadfast* is firm, unshakable, and unwavering. If you refuse to be comforted, you'll be weak, shaky, and wavering. God wants to use the troubles you face to transform you into a strong and mighty warrior with unshakable faith.

The more troubles you have, the more comfort God provides you through Christ. Notice it says he comforts you in "all" troubles. You won't face a single trouble that God won't comfort you through. He comforts you so you can be a comfort to others when they face troubles.

If you refuse to be comforted, then you'll deal with the pain and suffering indefinitely. In addition, you won't be any use to others who need comfort in their troubles. Further, you'll miss out on God's comfort and the sorrow will eventually produce death.

Godly sorrow brings repentance that leads to salvation and leaves
no regret, but worldly sorrow brings death.
(2 Corinthians 7:10 NIV)

Worldly sorrow is long-term. Depression is worldly sorrow. Regret is worldly sorrow. They lead to death. On your own, you can't overcome them by sheer willpower. The point is that Christ died and carried all your sorrow which provides you a way to deal with your sorrow and depression. You don't have to feel any of it—real or manufactured.

That is what I want for you from this book. I want you to learn how to give your sorrows and emotional pain over to Jesus. He already carried it whether you let Him or not. Donna could try to carry her bags even though I am willing to carry them for her. If she refused my help, she would have to carry the full burden. If she let me carry it for her, then it is no burden at all. She is free from it.

In the same way, if you simply let Jesus carry all your pain and sorrow and suffering, you will be free from it. You may be thinking that I don't know how deep the pain is. Maybe I don't. But Jesus does. He already knows how deep it is because He already carried it for you. There is no pain too deep that He can't heal. There is no sickness that is too difficult for Him to heal. His mercy is new every morning. Regardless of what happened to you yesterday, today is a new day, and God wants you to be free from the emotional pain of yesterday.

10

Freedom from Anxiety

Anxiety in the heart of man causes depression.
(Proverbs 12:25 NKJV)

In the previous chapter, we saw how debilitating depression can be. Depression is defined as severe despondency and dejection. The Bible says anxiety comes from the heart and causes depression. It's easy to see how that is true. Anxiety leads to fear, helplessness, and a feeling of doom. Prolonged anxiety leads to extreme sadness and a feeling that the circumstances are never going to end, or they are going to end in the worst possible outcome.

Let's see how anxiety caused David to sink into a deep depression.

I am troubled, I am bowed down greatly; I go mourning all the day
long. For my loins are full of inflammation, And there is no
soundness in my flesh. I am feeble and severely broken; I groan
because of the turmoil of my heart.
(Psalm 38:6-8 NKJV)

Anxiety is turmoil of the heart. David mourned because he couldn't resolve his turmoil. The depression was so severe, it caused him to become feeble and broken. He was in so much internal emotional pain, that it made him groan in agony. Medical studies have shown that when there's ongoing anxiety, it actually creates inflammation in your joints and in your brain. This inflammation leads to instability in your body and puts so much stress on your brain that it can result in depression.

David said this in another verse: My heart is severely pained within me, And the terrors of death have fallen upon me. Fearfulness and trembling have come upon me, And horror has overwhelmed me. So I said, "Oh, that I had wings like a dove! I would fly away and be at rest. (Psalm 55:4-6 NKJV)

David's anxiety was out of control. He was worried about death and his heart was severely pained. David instinctively knew that he needed rest. Not so much physical rest as emotional rest. He dreamed of flying away from his troubles like a dove, so he could get some relief.

Have you ever felt that way? Dreamed of flying away to a beach and soaking in the sun and getting away from all the cares of the world? That is something internal inside of us that instinctively knows when we need rest.

The Bible says we can be in that state of rest all the time. You don't have to fly away like a dove or be on a beach. Regardless of the circumstances, you can always have peace in your heart. That's because we have an advantage that David didn't have. The Holy Spirit lives inside us and gives us His fruit of the Spirit, one of which is peace. Peace is the opposite of anxiety. Rest is the result when peace comes into your life.

A movie came out in 1996 called *Twister*. Every few minutes was an intense scene where a tornado barreled down on panicked characters. Without fail, all of them ran as fast as they could to get to shelter where they could be protected. Except for the crazy storm chasers who tried to get closer to the tornado so they could study it. Though, even they rushed for safety when they got too close.

The troubles of the world are frightening and can create so much anxiety in you, that you must quickly enter the rest God has for you, so that you have peace even in the midst of the storm. Why is that so difficult to do? Why do so many Christians stay in the middle of the storm and cower in anxiety and depression rather than enter into the rest that God has provided for them?

It's because we don't understand why anxiety is not necessary.

A New Perspective on Anxiety

Several times a week, my wife and I hike a walking trail near our house. One part of the trail ventures into a heavily wooded area. One day we noticed a tree slightly off the trail that had what appeared to be a massive bee or wasp nest attached to one of its branches. Every time we walked by that area, we used extreme caution and hurried past the tree not wanting to do anything to stir up the bees.

This went on for several months. After a while I noticed that the nest never seemed to change size or appearance. I decided to get a closer look, but not without some trepidation. Turns out it wasn't a bee's nest at all. It was a large knot in the wood that looked like a hive All of our concern was for nothing. How foolish did we feel when we realized our mistake?

In the same way, so much of what we worry about in life is not real. Anxiety over past hurts is unnecessary. You can do nothing about the past other than not make the same mistakes in the present. I can see why many are anxious about future worries. Especially since we have already been warned by Jesus that we are going to have many troubles. If things are going well now, it's just a matter of time until trouble comes back into your life. That can certainly cause anxiety and worry about the unknown and what might happen in the future.

Yet the Bible is clear: *Be anxious for nothing.*

This verse says don't be anxious about anything. Not even future worries. There is not supposed to be one thing in this world that you are anxious about. How is that possible? The Bible wouldn't command us to do something that was impossible, so we need a new understanding.

The Greek word for *anxious* used in this passage has an interesting definition and tells us how it's possible to live worry free. The word means to be pulled apart, divided, and drawn in an opposite direction. It infers that anxiety is the act of being drawn away from the big picture.

In reality, that is what anxiety is. It's the sinful act of dividing your interests from the bigger picture, namely, taking your eyes off of the finished works of Christ and the hope of eternity that He is preparing for you and me. That's the big picture. Anxiety will disappear when you come to this truth: nothing on this earth can hurt you.

Sound crazy? Sound counterintuitive? Of course, there are many things in this world that can hurt you. That's not what Jesus said: And He said to them, "I saw Satan fall like lightning from heaven. Behold, I give you the authority to trample on serpents and scorpions, and over all the power of the enemy, and nothing shall by any means hurt you. (Luke 10: 18-19 NKJV)

Jesus had sent the disciples out into the world, two by two, to spread the gospel without Him. He knew He would eventually be crucified and go to heaven and someday and then they'd be on their own. This was a practice run, so to speak. The disciples came back extremely excited about their tremendous success. They were able to cast out demons and had power over the enemy to heal all manner of sickness and disease. The Lord had added thousands of believers to their cause and they were feeling invincible.

Jesus made an interesting statement which probably added to their confidence: *Nothing shall by any means hurt you.* In other words, the enemy has no power or any means in which to hurt you. The problem is that if you didn't know the context, you might think Jesus was saying something that wasn't true.

From a worldly standpoint, there are things on this earth that could hurt them. Each one of those disciples was martyred for the cause of Christ. They were beaten, thrown in prison, and suffered all types of humiliation and abuse of their physical bodies. Peter was even crucified upside down!

Yet, Jesus said that nothing can hurt them by any means. He was speaking of the big picture. Notice the rest of the verse: "Nevertheless do not rejoice in this, that the spirits are subject to you, but rather rejoice because your names are written in heaven." (Luke 10:20 NKJV)

Now you have the rest of the context. You have the big picture. Jesus was saying that nothing on this earth can hurt you if your names are written in heaven. If they were to rejoice in anything, they were to rejoice that they would spend an eternity in heaven with Jesus. From that perspective, there was nothing and no one on this earth who could take that away from them.

This wasn't the first time Jesus had made that point to them: "That is why I tell you not to worry about everyday life—whether you have enough food and drink, or enough clothes to wear. Isn't life more than food, and your body more than clothing? Look at the birds. They don't plant or harvest or store food in barns, for your heavenly Father feeds them. And aren't you far more valuable to him than they are? Can all your worries add a single moment to your life? (Matthew 6:25-27)

The bigger picture is represented in this verse. *Don't worry about your life.* What you eat or drink or what you will wear should not create any anxiety in you. *Isn't life more than food, and your body more than clothing?* If you look at the big picture, the only thing that really matters is that you will have an eternity with Christ. With that perspective, there is no reason to be anxious about anything related to earthly things.

Of course, Jesus said that God would even supply all of our needs according to His riches in glory.[9] So we don't even have to be anxious about the necessities of life. God will provide those just as He provides them for the birds and the flowers.

Once your eternal destination is secure, you can always rejoice. If you come to that realization, then you can always feel peace. You can always rejoice regardless of what happens, good or bad. Here is how it works:

You may have trouble. Don't worry. Your name is written in heaven.

You may get cancer. There's no reason to fear cancer. It can't really hurt you. Your name is written in heaven.

You may have sinned and are facing the consequences of it. Rejoice. Your name is written in heaven.

Your house was foreclosed on. Don't worry about it. Your name is written in heaven.

You are persecuted for His name's sake. Thrown in jail. Beaten. Stoned to death. It doesn't matter. Your name is written in heaven.

With that perspective, you will realize that there is nothing anyone can do to take your peace. There is nothing on this earth that can cause anxiety. There is nothing the enemy can do to hurt you if your name is written in heaven.

What a powerful truth! Nothing on this earth can hurt you. Not even COVID-19 can harm you. It can take your life, but it can't remove your name from the Lamb's Book of Life. Thieves can rob and loot your home and steal your possessions. They can't touch the mansion Jesus is preparing for you in heaven.

Here is how I approached the global pandemic. It's based on several Bible verses.

1. I can't get it.

Psalm 91 tells me not to be afraid of the deadly pestilence: You shall not be afraid of the terror by night, Nor of the arrow that flies by day, Nor of the pestilence that walks in darkness, Nor of the destruction that lays waste at noonday.

Other verses say that angels watch over us and protect us from any deadly pestilence that might strike the world.

2. If I do get it, God will heal me. He himself bore our sicknesses. (Isaiah 53:4)

I live my life with the belief that Jesus bore my sicknesses on the cross, and therefore, if I get sick, He has provided healing for my body. So, I don't worry about COVID. If I get it, God will heal me.

3. If God doesn't heal me, He'll use it for my good. And we know that all things work together for good to those who love God, to those who are called according to His purpose. (Romans 8:28)

This verse says God will work all things for my good. *All* means all and includes COVID. Therefore, I can have peace knowing that even if I get the disease, God will use it for my good.

4. If I die, I get to go to heaven sooner which is better. For to me, to live is Christ, and to die is gain. (Philippians 1:21)

Paul said in another verse that we are all better off in heaven with Jesus. He preferred to die and go to heaven as opposed to living in this sinful world. The only reason he was willing to stay was because God was using him. When God was through with his mission, then he wanted to go be with the Lord.

If you have that point of view, you will not be afraid of death or any deadly pestilence. Believing the Bible is true gives you the renewed mind to trust God and not worry about the things of the world that cause anxiety to those who don't know God.

That is the big picture. Anxiety is an emotion that turns your focus away from the big picture. It divides your attention from what is of eternal importance. Whenever you feel anxiety, as quickly and diligently as possible, you must labor to get back to a place of peace.

Don't Worry, God Will Help You

Truthfully, you can't get to the place of worry-free on your own. A life free from anxiety, takes supernatural help from God. Medication can certainly help and is necessary in some cases. Certain breathing techniques can lessen anxiety. Even a vacation on a beach can bring some relief. However, true freedom comes from God.

> I am leaving you with a gift—peace of mind and heart. And the peace I give is a gift the world cannot give. So don't be troubled or afraid.
> (John 14:27)

Peace of mind and heart is a free gift from Jesus. The world cannot give you anything similar to it. Peace is available to everyone who receives it therefore you have no reason to be troubled or afraid. You can walk free from the toxic emotions linked to darkness and experience the fruit of the Spirit anywhere and anytime. It is a free gift. It's not something you have to earn. All you must do is receive.

Good works can't buy you this kind of peace. The world can't give you peace of mind and heart. You don't have to become a better person to enter into the rest God is promising you in this life. The only requirement is to believe, confess, and receive. This is the promise of God. You can have total peace. You can walk in immediate abundance. However, you must "let" Jesus do it for you.

> And **let** the peace of God rule in your hearts, to which also you were called in one body; and be thankful
> (Colossians 3:15 NKJV Emphasis added).

The word *rule* in this verse is similar to how an umpire in baseball rules. He determines if a batter is safe or out. Peace is a fruit of the Spirit that can help you make decisions. Emotions were designed to give you information. Feelings can give you a perspective on a situation. They can also help you make decisions. If you feel peace about a decision, then you should make it. If you don't feel peace, you should hold off. Peace is not an emotion, but it provokes emotions in you. You may have feelings of discontent or uneasiness when the Holy Spirit is trying to tell you that you need to change your circumstances.

If you let peace rule, it means God's peace is stronger than the negative emotions and rules over them. The Greek word for *rule* actually means a standard of measure. It's where we get the word, "ruler." In other words, peace is the standard of measure in your heart. Everything is measured against peace. If it's not peace, it must subject itself to peace and come under its control and domination. Peace is only one fruit of the Spirit, but the same principle applies to all; you must let the fruit of the Spirit be free to flow from your spirit into your flesh through your mind.

> Let not your heart be troubled; you believe in God, believe also in Me. (John 14:1 KJV)

Notice how many times the Bible uses the word "let" when it is talking about peace and overcoming anxiety. Don't let your heart be troubled. Let peace rule your heart. Let your requests be made known to God. The word *let* means to allow or to permit. Don't permit your heart to be troubled; instead, permit God to give you His peace.

How do you let God give you peace? What is the process? You make your requests known to God.

> Be anxious for nothing, but in everything by prayer and supplication, with thanksgiving, let your requests be made known to God; and the peace of God, which surpasses all understanding, will guard your hearts and minds through Christ Jesus.
> (Philippians 4:6-7 NKJV)

This verse outlines the process.

1. Say a prayer.
2. Give thanks.
3. Let your requests be made known to God.

There are two things to remember. One is that your circumstances may not change. The Bible verse says to make your requests known to God, and He will give you peace. It doesn't say God will change your circumstances. Like the disciples, you will face troubles, but nothing can hurt you.

The other thing to remember is that feelings are temporary. They are supposed to only last for a short period of time. Anxiety lasts for a long time because we hold on to it. We don't let it go. If you will let go of the past hurts and future worries, you can find rest. Then when present troubles come on you, take heart in knowing that your name is written in heaven.

11

Freedom from Discontentment

The Bible is often extremely accurate in describing how the past affected a person's present condition and even in documenting how long a person had been suffering from his/her infirmity. The blind man was "blind from birth" (John 9:1). The invalid laid by the pool for "thirty-eight" years (John 5:5). The woman was "bent over" for eighteen years (Luke 13:11). Lazarus had been dead and in the tomb for "four days" (John 11:17). Mary Magdalene was delivered from "seven" spirits (Luke 8:2). The woman with the issue of blood had suffered for "twelve years" (Luke 8:43). Notice that the Bible specifically says what the person was suffering from and how long they had been suffering.

While God is not bound by time and space, His promises are when they are specific to us. Very few of God's directives happen immediately, but they will happen within a determined time frame if certain conditions are met. Generally, a period of waiting follows His Words allowing for the testing of the person's faith.

We only receive God's promises when faith is applied to them. Any of God's promises that are not mixed with faith, will not profit us. Time is used to test faith. Patience is the proof of faith.

Patience is a fruit of the Spirit and is required if we don't receive the promises immediately. The Greek word for *patience* is long suffering or endurance. This signifies time and also infers that suffering may be involved. God tests our faith by seeing if we still believe after a period of time has passed. Notice the passage of time in the following examples of testing of faith from the Bible:

- Instantly: Mark 10:52. Jesus healed the blind man instantly.

- Few Minutes or Hours: John 9:7. The blind man was healed after he followed the instructions of Jesus and washed in the pool of Siloam.

- Three Days: Acts 9:9. Paul was blinded on the road to Damascus. Ananias laid hands on him three days later, and he was healed.

- Jonah was in the belly of the whale for three days and three nights.

- Forty Days: Jesus fasted forty days in the wilderness and faced three temptations from Satan.

- Forty Days and Forty Nights: It rained for forty days and forty nights while Noah and his family survived in the ark.

- Two Years: Paul was in a Roman prison for two years.

- Twelve Years: The woman with the issue of blood suffered for twelve years.

- Twenty-five Years: Abraham was promised a son even though he was old, but it took twenty-five years before the promise was fulfilled.

- Forty years: Children of Israel were promised a land flowing of milk and honey. They wandered in the wilderness for forty years before they were allowed to go in, and only two of the original group were allowed to enter.

- One Hundred Twenty years: God told Noah that he was going to flood the earth, and Noah was instructed to build an ark even though there wasn't a cloud in the sky. It was approximately one hundred twenty years before the flood came. It took Noah roughly fifty-five to seventy years to complete the work on the ark.

■ Four Hundred Thirty-Eight years: Children of Israel were slaves in Egypt. They were promised a deliverer, but it took four hundred thirty-eight years before God raised up Moses and they were delivered from slavery.

As you can see, there's a big difference in the amount of time between trials. They range from instant healing to four hundred thirty-eight years. Time tests faith because genuine faith will last as long as necessary. What if Noah had given up building the ark after fifty years? He would have perished with everyone else. Steadfast faithfulness over time is the proof of faith.

What happens if you don't maintain your faith through the entire time frame?

My brethren, count it all joy when you fall into various trials, knowing that the testing of your faith produces patience. But let patience have its perfect work, that you may be perfect and complete, lacking nothing. If any of you lacks wisdom, let him ask of God, who gives to all liberally and without reproach, and it will be given to him. But let him ask in faith, with no doubting, for he who doubts is like a wave of the sea driven and tossed by the wind. For let not that man suppose that he will receive anything from the Lord; he is a double-minded man, unstable in all his ways. (James 1:2-8 NKJV)

We are to respond with joy to various trials. Why is that? Because we know that the testing of our faith produces patience, which is a fruit of the Spirit, and joy is our way of letting God know we believe His Word. Without time passing, patience is unnecessary. Patience has a purpose. It must do its "perfect work" in us. When patience is allowed to work in our lives, we become complete, whole, and lack nothing.

How would you like to lack nothing? God's promises can only become a reality in your life and "profit" you when enough time has passed to produce patience in you. If you lack faith, then it will be exposed over time. Remember that God is not bound by time and can see into the future. If He knows that your faith has a breaking point or a time in the future when you will give up hope and doubt God's promises, then God can see that in advance and withhold the promise even though your faith may be strong in the moment.

This verse should be sobering, but instructive, to all of us. A double minded man doubts before patience can finish the work. That person should not expect to receive "anything from the Lord."

Discontentment Breeds Doubt

Discontent means to be dissatisfied with your current circumstances and is the opposite of patience. Discontentment is the state of being discontent. It is an emotion that robs you of seeing the fulfillment of the promises of God in your life because it causes you to give up on God's promises before they have time to manifest.

It's not unlike a woman with child. She must wait the full nine months to give birth. As uncomfortable as it is, or as much as she wants to shortcut the process and have the child earlier, the nine months is needed for the child to be ready to be born. In a similar way, God's promises are growing inside of us and will not be birthed until God is ready for them. Therefore, we must wait on them and be content until they come.

I have learned how to be content with whatever I have. I know how to live on almost nothing or with everything. I have learned the secret of living in every situation, whether it is with a full stomach or empty, with plenty or little. For I can do everything through Christ who gives me strength. (Philippians 4:11-13)

Paul said that he was content with whatever he had. He tells us the reason why he was always content. He was never in need. Discontentment is a belief that you are lacking something that you need. Impatience demands that God act now because you are discontented with your current situation. Paul came to understand that he always had everything he needed through Christ who gave him strength. He called it the "secret" of living.

Paul had an unconditional belief that God would supply all his needs through Christ Jesus. If you believe that fact, you will never be discontented. Discontentment is unbelief. Paul was always content in his circumstances because he always trusted God.

Discontent becomes a toxic emotion when it lingers beyond an immediate decision. Discontent is not meant to become a continual state of mind. When used as God intended, discontent can become a conviction that will motivate you to change something that needs to be changed in your life. If that discontentment is the Spirit of God trying to get you to change something in your life, then it is a positive emotion.

Ongoing feelings of discontent that turns to unhappiness can lead you to make bad decisions. If discontentment grows into dissatisfaction with what God has given you or into a constant feeling of discontent with your life, a bad decision may result. Many people leave their marriages, jobs, and other relationships because of discontentment. They allow discontentment to be an ongoing emotion that builds over time.

Discontentment that leads to unhappiness can become so consuming an emotion that you are unhappy all the time. It becomes toxic when you think your circumstances are the problem and that if you change them, then you will feel content. If the discontent is from a toxic emotion that lingers then it doesn't matter if you change your circumstances; the discontent will eventually return or never really go away.

Have you ever heard someone say, "I hate my life, I hate my job, or I hate my marriage?" Their discontent has become toxic. Paul was determined to never let those thoughts get a foothold in his emotions. Let's see how Paul practiced what he preached:

> Then the multitude rose up together against them; and the magistrates tore off their clothes and commanded them to be beaten with rods. And when they had laid many stripes on them, they threw them into prison, commanding the jailer to keep them securely. Having received such a charge, he put them into the inner prison and fastened their feet in the stocks. But at midnight Paul and Silas were praying and singing hymns to God, and the prisoners were listening to them. (Acts 16:22-25 NKJV)

It's hard to imagine a worse situation for Paul and Silas. They were beaten with rods nearly to death and then thrown into prison. Their feet were fastened to stocks. The conditions had to be deplorable for someone with open wounds on his body.

Yet, despite their trouble, at the midnight hour which is the darkest time in the night, Paul and Silas were praying and singing hymns to God! What a testimony of faith and an example of how to handle present troubles. If Paul could be content in that situation, he could be content in anything. He wasn't grumbling and complaining and feeling sorry for himself. He wasn't demanding that

God free him from that situation immediately.

Paul's response was the opposite of how most of us would respond. He responded with joy, just as he had encouraged others to do in his writings. They weren't worried or afraid. Sadness and depression were nowhere to be found in that prison cell. They were rejoicing and trusting God and praying to God. They didn't even wait until the morning for joy to come; they started rejoicing immediately.

Shortly after midnight, God sent an earthquake, and they were released from their chains and the prison doors were opened. Because of their faith, God was able to move immediately. "Suddenly" an earthquake came and loosed their chains. God didn't need to wait for months or years to see if Paul would be patient and wait with joy for Him to act. He knew immediately that Paul's faith would not be shaken. So, a trial wasn't necessary to test Paul's faith.

Shortly after midnight, the Scripture says an earthquake freed them from their chains and opened the door to their cell. A miracle happened, the jailer and his family were saved, and Paul and Silas were taken out of prison, fed at the jailer's house, and their wounds were treated. Not only were they not angry at their captor; they witnessed to him and led him to salvation.

This response had to come from a deep belief that God was good and would take care of them. Even if they hadn't been miraculously delivered out of the jail cell, they were already delivered from the toxic emotions they could have felt because they were filled with joy because of their faith.

This is what can happen to you. Trouble can come on you at any time. Suddenly, with no notice you can have your foundations shaken and your life turned upside down. You may have legitimate reasons to feel negative emotions. Paul and Silas certainly did. However, they did not let their emotions dictate how they felt about

God. I am speculating, but if they had been overcome with emotions and were angry at God or fearful or anxious that they were going to die, God probably would not have sent the earthquake to free them from their chains.

When you respond to circumstances with fear, anger, depression, anxiety, and toxic emotions, you make it harder for God to help you through your circumstances. When you respond by faith and with praise and worship and rejoicing, God can suddenly respond and free you from your troubles. Once you are free from your toxic emotions, God is free to resolve your troubles which He promised He would do.

Impatience Leads to Complaining and Questioning

Remember the verse that a double minded man is unstable in all his ways and should not expect anything from God. Impatience is double mindedness. It is an emotion based on underlying unbelief. Unbelief is the kryptonite that destroys faith and keeps God from answering your prayers.

Do all things without complaining and disputing.
(Philippians 2:14 NKJV)

When impatient emotions are not controlled, complaining and disputing is the end result. The word *disputing* means questioning. The word *questioning* means to raise doubt. When you complain out of your impatience, you are saying to God that you doubt Him. Again, that double-minded person should expect nothing from God.

There are two truths that must become self-evident in your life and be the foundation of everything you do and say:

1. God is good.
2. God never lies.

If you believe these two truths, then they can become the pillars of patience. If God is good and never lies, then you can wait on Him to act on your behalf, knowing He will always do what is best for you.

I first learned this lesson as a teenager. At an early age, I started teaching myself how to play the guitar. My first instrument was an old Gibson that my dad had used for many years. It had seen better days. I was starting to become good at it and had opportunities to play at churches. I desperately wanted a new guitar and begged my parents for one.

One day I went into a music store and found what I thought was the perfect guitar. I told my parents about it, and their response was that I had to wait. At some point they would get me a new guitar, but not then. I badgered my parents to the point they almost bought me that guitar just to shut me up.

I'm so thankful they didn't. Three months later, my parents surprised me with a new guitar. A friend of theirs owned a music store. He told them that I could pick out any guitar in the store I wanted at cost. The guitar was beyond what I could've ever imagined or asked for and was significantly better than the other guitar I had badgered my parents for, and it cost them less because their friend gave it to them at cost.

I played that guitar at their church that Sunday morning and was ecstatic. I've had that guitar for years, and it is a constant reminder to me of God's faithfulness and that patience is rewarded. If I wait for God's blessings, they will always be better than the outcome I am trying to manufacture through my impatience.

The opposite of impatience is endurance. The Greek word *endurance* is the same word as the one used for patience. We must run the race of life set before us with patience. It's a marathon, not a sprint. The race is best run without weights. Imagine running a marathon with ankle weights. It makes the race almost impossible to run.

Toxic emotions are like weights around our ankles that slow us down. And we should know better. We have a great cloud of witnesses to look to for strength. The Bible is full of individual stories of people who we can learn from and draw strength and inspiration. Even in our own lives, we can all look back on a time when God was faithful. Like the guitar, I've had many instances where God has proven Himself to me to the point that I don't need to doubt His goodness or His honesty.

That is why I can run the race with patience. The guitar lesson was a simple one. Now as an adult, I've had instances in my life where my patience has produced tremendous blessings from God. I've also had circumstances where my impatience has cost me relationships, time, and money. My life is always better when I wait with joy on God.

As the Word of God implores, you must "Lay aside" the weight of discontentment. If you can get to where you are content in everything, like Paul was, then you can have joy no matter what the circumstance. It's the best way to live.

12

Freedom from Anger

Admittedly, the principles in this book seem impossible to implement perfectly in your life. That's because the Bible sets an impossible standard in every area and sets a high bar that we can all only strive to achieve. Paul said in Romans that God established the Old Testament law to show us that we weren't good enough to meet it. Jesus said if you break one of the laws, you've broken them all. His harshest words were for the Pharisees who pretended to obey them on the outside, but their hearts were evil like everyone else's.

Such are the impossible emotional standards outlined in this book. Not grieving over the death of a loved one seems counterintuitive. Freedom from anxiety, depression, and other toxic emotions may seem like a pipe dream to you, that are unrealistic, and may only cause more frustration if you don't understand the reason why God gave us these standards of emotional perfection. In this chapter, I hope to explain the reason more fully as we understand the purpose for anger and how we can overcome it in the way the Bible instructs.

After teaching these concepts at a Bible study, one lady was angry at me. She was even angry at God. She said, "That's so unfair that God would expect us to get over the loss of a loved one in one day!" She was emphatic in her criticism of the teaching and the Bible verses that supported it.

The truth is that you don't have to be free from toxic emotions over the loss of a loved one, you just can be. We all live under the new covenant of grace. God is not going to judge you for struggling with emotions. At the same time, Jesus made a wonderful provision for emotional freedom, knowing that we can't handle emotions on our own. Freedom, therefore, is a choice. You can choose to continue to suffer in your emotional pain, or you can choose to believe God and let His Spirit replace your emotions with fruit. Namely, the wonderful fruit of the Spirit that brings comfort and peace.

That being said, this chapter isn't going to make emotional freedom sound any easier to accomplish. The Bible gives three seemingly impossible instructions related to anger:

1. Be angry but don't sin. (Ephesians 4:26)

2. Be slow to anger. (James 1:19)

3. Be over it before sundown. (Ephesians 4:26)

What would the world be like if everyone followed those three principles? There would be no wars. Most prisons would be empty. Murders, assaults, rapes, and crimes of passion would be nonexistent. Divorce court dockets would be empty. Child protective services would have nothing to do and no children to protect. Of all the emotions, anger is the one that contributes the most to the destructive decline of our society.

Why do we have such an angry society? The Bible never tells us not to be angry. It just says not to sin in our anger. You only have to turn on the television to see people sinning in their anger at every turn.

Anger is an emotion from God. The Bible says many times that God gets angry. The Bible also says that God cannot sin. Therefore, anger in and of itself is not sin. When is it not? When it is appropriate. Anger was given to us by God to respond to an injustice. Righteous indignation is anger over mistreatment, abuse, or immorality and is the only anger that is not a sin.

Jesus modeled righteous indignation when He drove out the moneychangers in the Temple. As we have seen previously, even that anger was temporary and resolved the same day the anger surfaced. Anger directed toward another person that is designed to hurt that person is sin. Jesus even said in Matthew 5:21 that anger toward another brother is like committing murder in your heart.

The truth is that sinful people are going to hurt each other. The Bible calls them "offenses." So does the criminal justice system. When laws are broken, an offense has occurred. An offense is defined as an illegal act. It is also a wrong committed against another person that might not be illegal but is hurtful.

Jesus said there are two laws we should live by and sets the standard even higher than our laws. He said we are to love God, love our neighbor, and love ourselves. If you think about it, every emotional root and toxic emotion can be tied to a deficit of love. The root of anger is tied to a lack of love for someone. Resentment, bitterness, jealousy, envy, covetousness, loneliness, and revenge are all based on unforgiveness and a lack of love toward someone who hurt you in your past. Guilt, shame, and condemnation are rooted in a lack of love for yourself. You literally despise yourself for something you did in the past.

How are emotional roots broken? They are broken through love. Love is the impetus for forgiveness. If someone has offended you, if you love them, you will forgive them. If they are unlovable, then you forgive them because you love God and because God has forgiven you. Finally, you forgive yourself because God has forgiven you and because you love who you are in Christ.

Love is the Round-Up for emotional roots. It kills them on the spot. It is impossible to feel negative, toxic, and destructive emotions and feel love at the same time. They cannot coexist in your heart. Love is listed as the first fruit of the Spirit. Then joy, then peace. Love is the foundation for joy and peace.

So, what is that fine line between appropriate anger and sin? In the same chapter where we are told to be angry but do not sin, the Bible lists a number of offenses someone can do to us, such as lying, stealing, and corrupt words:

> Therefore, putting away lying, "Let each one of you speak truth with his neighbor," for we are members of one another. "Be angry, and do not sin": do not let the sun go down on your wrath, nor give place to the devil. Let him who stole steal no longer, but rather let him labor, working with his hands what is good, that he may have something to give him who has need. Let no corrupt word proceed out of your mouth, but what is good for necessary edification, that it may impart grace to the hearers. And do not grieve the Holy Spirit of God, by whom you were sealed for the day of redemption. Let all bitterness, wrath, anger, clamor, and evil speaking be put away from you, with all malice. And be kind to one another, tenderhearted, forgiving one another, even as God in Christ forgave you. (Ephesians 4:25-32 NKJV)

The context of anger in these verses is related to offenses. Lying to your neighbor is an offense that provokes anger. Stealing from your neighbors will justifiably make them angry. Corrupt words, slander, gossip, words spoken in malice, are all offenses between us that cause the emotion of anger to rise inside of us. The result is bitterness, wrath, anger, clamor, and evil speaking.

What are we instructed to do with that anger? The Bible says to put it away from you. That means to get rid of it as soon as possible so it is not even a part of your being. Then it tells you how to respond to the offense: With kindness and forgiveness. Kindness is the fruit of the Spirit that is the opposite of anger.

Have you ever noticed that the ways of God are opposite to the ways of the world? The reason that the principles of this book seem impossible, is because they are the opposite from how our sinful nature wants to respond. When someone lies to us, our normal response is to lash out in anger. When somebody steals our money or possessions, anger seems like the appropriate response.

Even in the most egregious offenses, the Bible says our anger is to be resolved the same day the offense occurs. Think of that in practical terms. You discover your spouse is having an affair. That may seem like the ultimate offense to many who are reading this. I've heard spouses describe it as the unforgivable sin. It can certainly be a painful and devastating event that can shake your entire world.

The Bible instructs that if that happens to you, your anger is to be resolved on the same day you learn of it, and the hurt and sorrow should be resolved and turned to joy by the next morning.

Oh, come on!

How is that even possible? At the risk of causing you to close this book and never reopen it, I must make the argument that the Bible doesn't command us to do something that is impossible. Not only is it possible; it is what God wants for you. He knows that if your anger is allowed to carry beyond a day and your sorrows last beyond the night, then a root of bitterness can establish itself in your heart and turn into a toxic emotion. Jesus died to prevent that from happening. Then He sent the Holy Spirit, the Comforter, to live inside of us, so we would always have a way to resolve the emotional pain, no matter how devastating it might appear to be.

> Looking carefully lest anyone fall short of the grace of God; lest any root of bitterness springing up cause trouble, and by this many become defiled. (Hebrews 12:15 NKJV)

This verse puts anger into a sobering perspective. When we don't respond to someone else's offense with kindness and forgiveness, then we fall short of the grace of God. When that happens, we become defiled. The Greek word for *defiled* means stained. It also means contaminated. When we let sin enter our lives in the form of sexual impurity, adultery, lying, and stealing, those offenses contaminate and stain our bodies whose spirits have been redeemed by the spirit of God. So does responding to the offense with anger.

Every offense provides two opportunities for contamination and sin. One by the person who commits the offense; the other by the person who was offended who responds in anger and allows a root of bitterness to stain his mortal body.

You saw earlier in the book how anger is listed with sins such as sexual immorality, idolatry, drunkenness, and other serious sins. Quarrelling, hostility, jealousy, outbursts of anger, dissension, division, and envy, are on the same list as drunkenness, orgies, sorcery, and idolatry. That should cause everyone to pause. We are all quick to judge the adulterer while being sympathetic to the one cheated on. The Bible says both are following after the desires of their sinful natures.

The next time someone offends you, you should think twice before responding in judgement and anger. You will fall short of the grace of God that is a free gift to everyone who believes.

What is the Appropriate Response to an Offense?

Or do you show contempt for the riches of his kindness,
forbearance and patience, not realizing that God's kindness is
intended to lead you to repentance?
(Romans 2:4 NIV)

To paraphrase this verse, are you aware that it is God's kindness that led *you* to repentance? All have sinned and fallen short of the glory of God. Anyone who claims to have not sinned, is fooling himself, and the love of God is not in Him. Those two verses confirm what we should already know: We all need God's grace.

Your anger toward another person who has offended and wronged you, no matter how grievous, deserves the same kindness, forbearance, and patience that you receive from God. We all live under the covenant of grace. We all deserve judgment and hell. A person is arrogant who thinks that they have the right to receive grace from God when they offend others, but they aren't going to give it to someone else when they themselves are offended.

At the same time, when one of us sins, we deserve the same grace from each other that God has given to us freely through the finished works of Christ. When we respond in anger, we show contempt for the kindness of God that is trying to lead that person back to repentance. Our vitriol and harsh words do nothing but circumvent what God is trying to do to restore that person back to a right relationship with Him. He is trying to help that person with kindness; we are often standing in the way with our anger and bitterness.

> Brethren, if a man is overtaken in any trespass, you who are spiritual restore such a one in a spirit of gentleness, considering yourself lest you also be tempted. (Galatians 6:1 NKJV)

Our first response to someone else's sin, should be gentleness, not anger. Kindness not bitterness. Encouragement not judgment. Considering such, knowing that at some point you may also be tempted and offend someone else and be in need of gentleness.

> Most important of all, continue to show deep love for each other, for love covers a multitude of sins. (1 Peter 4:8)

This verse says that love is the most important thing of all. Loving another when he has sinned and has offended you is the most important thing you can do. Showing deep love for another person who doesn't deserve it is above everything else you can do as a Christian. Your love will actually cover their sin. Most people want to expose the person who offended them. Gossip and tell others about their shortcomings. Love actually attempts to cover the sin with grace.

Love is a fruit of the Spirit. You must let the fruit of the Spirit flow from your spirit to your flesh and manifest in love for the other person. You need to "let" love take control of the emotional roots.

Let your love be genuine.
(Romans 12:9 ESV)

Let love and faithfulness never leave you.
(Proverbs 3:3-4 NIV)

Let us love one another.
(1 John 4: 7 NIV)

There's that word "let" again. It's something we have to let God do inside of us. Our normal response is anger; we have to let the love of God overtake that anger.

Don't misunderstand this teaching. Sinning has consequences. You may not choose to stay married to someone who has broken their vows and entered into an adulterous relationship. If someone has lied or stolen from you, or committed any such grievous offense, I am not saying that you have to take it and allow them to do it again and again. The consequences may be severe for those actions. Law enforcement may even need to be involved.

I am talking about how you respond emotionally. Prudence and wisdom may cause you to take actions to protect yourself. Responding with kindness is protecting your own heart. A root of bitterness that is allowed to grow inside of you, will damage you more than it damages the other person. It cuts off the flow of grace in your life that you so desperately need at times.

When you look at it from this perspective, then the appropriate emotional response is possible. Even something as potentially emotionally hurtful as an affair. Your refusal to be angry, your insistence on responding in kindness, provides the best atmosphere for that person to repent and be restored to a right relationship with God.

That is the goal. Hurting that person through anger and harsh words produces guilt, shame, and condemnation in them, which plays right into the enemy's hands. When you respond to an offense with kindness and forgiveness, those are the times that you are most like God.

13

Freedom from Shame

There is none who does good, no, not one.

(Romans 3:12 NKJV)

The next fruit of the Spirit on the list is goodness. According to the Bible, we are incapable of doing good. Because of our sinful natures imputed to us at the fall—almost as if it is in our DNA—we are habitually falling short of the glory of God and are deserving of the guilt we feel and the punishment that we should face. Therefore, this chapter must tackle another seemingly impossible task: How do we overcome the emotional consequences of our sin? Namely, guilt, condemnation, and shame.

> David said what we have all felt at one time or another: I live in disgrace all day long, and my face is covered with shame.
> (Psalm 44:15 NIV)

A video is circulating social media of a snake who had wrapped his body around a handsaw thinking it was prey. He was attempting to squeeze the life out of the saw not realizing that he was only hurting himself. Eventually, he squeezed so hard that his body was cut in two and he died.

That is what the toxic emotion of shame does to a believer. It slowly squeezes the abundant life out of his soul. The wound is self-inflicted. Not that we don't deserve it. Shame is the byproduct of sin. A person sins and feels guilt. The guilt brings on condemnation. The condemnation causes feelings of shame.

When Adam and Eve sinned in the garden, the emotion they felt was shame. Their natural instinct was to hide from God. Instinctively, they felt guilt and knew they had done something wrong. They hid because they knew they were condemned to punishment. They felt shame because they had let God down and were unsure what the consequences would be.

Guilt, condemnation, and shame are the consequences of sin. They are the "normal" results of walking in the flesh and allowing sinful desires to overcome what you know is the right thing to do. The verse at the beginning of this chapter says that no one does good, not a single person, so shame is inevitable.

In the Old Covenant, shame was rampant and there was no real mechanism to resolve it. The emphasis in these Bible verses are mine.

Jeremiah 17:13 NIV: Lord, you are the hope of Israel; all who forsake you will be put to *shame*.

Ezekiel 43:10 NIV: Son of man, describe the temple to the people of Israel, that they may be *ashamed* of their sins.

Ezra 9:6 NIV: I am too *ashamed* and disgraced, my God, to lift up my face to you, because our sins are higher than our heads and our guilt has reached to the heavens.

Psalm 69:19 NIV: You know how I am scorned, disgraced and *shamed*; all my enemies are before you.

The people living under the old covenant knew full well what sin was and what the consequences were because they were spelled out in the law. Punishments for various sins and guilt were ascribed to their actions when they "broke" the law. In our court of law, people are declared guilty all the time. It simply means they did break the law and are deserving of punishment.

The emotion of guilt can be useful to a believer. Guilt says you did something bad. When it's conviction of sin it is not entirely a bad thing. It's good to realize that you have done something that you didn't want to do, or you shouldn't have done. Self-awareness is realizing that some behaviors fall short of how you want to live your life.

It becomes toxic when it evolves into shame. While guilt says that you did something bad, shame says that you are a bad person. Shame is devastating emotionally. The Bible already says you are a bad person, so shame is normal and expected.

Shame is a negative and intense feeling of self-loathing. It devalues self. It's a feeling of unworthiness, regret, and that you are deserving of punishment. It makes you feel like you are flawed, and that God must be mad at you for doing something so bad. It leads to the display of negative emotions including envy, rage, anger, anxiety, sadness, loneliness, emptiness, and depression. It leads to a self-belief that if people really knew you and what you have done, they would be appalled.

Shame is overwhelming. It consumes your life and can be so intense, it can lead to suicidal thoughts, abuse, and severe depression and anxiety. It often causes you to want to hide, to withdraw from others and isolate yourself from hurting yourself again by doing something else that is bad.

Shame affects your relationships. Shame makes you feel like you are defective and unworthy of love. Feelings of shame cause you to lash out at others and find fault in them so that you can feel better about yourself. Shame tends to direct people to destructive behaviors. Most eating disorders and addictions come from a poor self-image. Drugs and alcohol are often just ways to cope with the shame. It goes away for a short period of time but then comes back even stronger with more shame because the person feels even worse because of the addiction.

Women, in particular, make decisions in relationships based on their own self-image. They tend to choose people that they think they deserve. If they feel like they are a bad person, then all they deserve is to be with someone else who is as bad or worse than they are. Those feelings of unworthiness often cause women to give themselves sexually to someone just so they can feel loved. That sin just leads to more shame.

And it is all deserved. Every one of us deserves guilt, condemnation, and feelings of shame.

We Don't Get What We Deserve

My wife, Donna, is the best clothes shopper I know. If there were a prize for the closet with the best-looking clothes at the most economical price, she would win hands down. She has a knack for finding bargain dresses, shoes, shirts, and pants that look spectacular on her. She gets so excited when she finds a dress at TJ Maxx for seven dollars on the clearance rack. Honestly, I can't tell the difference between a TJ Maxx dress and a designer dress worn by a Hollywood star who spent hundreds of dollars on it.

One of her strategies is that she is in their rewards programs. She frequently gets reward certificates in the mail that offer her big discounts. She gets two types of rewards. One is a percentage off reward. For instance, she recently got a $30.00 Super Cash Reward voucher from Old Navy. If she buys $75.00 worth of items, she receives $30.00 off her purchase with the reward's voucher.

The best rewards certificates give her a dollar-for-dollar discount. She recently got a $40.00 certificate off any purchase at TJ Maxx. She can go into the store and buy any item worth $40.00 or less, and she will get that item for free. Most of her closet is filled with discounted items that didn't cost her anything!

The Bible also contains two different reward systems. They are like the ones I described above, only the rewards aren't clothes, they're eternal life. One reward system was the old covenant which was in place before Jesus died. It's like the Old Navy voucher that gives you a discount if you buy something, meaning it's conditional. Just like the store discount is conditional on you buying a certain dollar amount of clothes, the old covenant was conditional upon man keeping God's commandments and laws. If man was obedient, he received the rewards, and God blessed him in his health, finances, marriage, and relationships.

> But now He has obtained a more excellent ministry, inasmuch as He is also Mediator of a better covenant, which was established on better promises. (Hebrews 8:6 NKJV)

When Christ died, a new covenant was established based on grace received through faith. These are based on new and better promises. It's like the TJ Maxx $40.00 reward. You can redeem it with no strings attached. All you have to do is believe and it is yours. However, if you don't believe it, you will never receive it.

To illustrate, let's say that Donna received a $40.00 unconditional reward from TJ Maxx. She could redeem it anytime for $40.00 worth of clothes, no strings attached. What if she didn't believe that the reward was real and never tried to cash it in? She would never receive the reward. What if she didn't believe that the reward really gave her $40.00 in purchasing power, so she only bought $10.00 worth of clothes? Either way, she would never have taken advantage of what was available to her.

In the same way, most Christians are not accessing the full rewards of the new covenant. Most believe Christ died for our sins. It is the basis of our faith, and the reward for believing in Christ is eternal life. However, most don't realize that Christ also died for all our emotional problems. Before we get to that, let's look at the verses that show us that Christ died for our sins.

> For the wages of sin is death, but the gift of God is eternal life in
> Christ Jesus our Lord.
> (Romans 6:23 NKJV)

There is another powerful three-letter word in that sentence. The word "but." We all deserve death but... Everyone deserves to feel shame but... The word "but" nullifies what precedes it with what follows it.

> But now God has shown us a way to be made right with him
> without keeping the requirements of the law, as was
> promised in the writings of Moses and the prophets long ago.
> We are made right with God by placing our faith in Jesus
> Christ. And this is true for everyone who believes, no matter
> who we are. (Romans 3:21-22)

What a remarkable passage of Scripture! Jesus Christ, on the cross, took away all your sin and made you right in God's sight. If you are right in God's sight, He is no longer mad at you. If He were, He would have to apologize to Christ. Christ voluntarily took your sins and your guilt upon Himself even though He was without sin. He sacrificed Himself so that you could be in right standing with God. Because you are in right standing with God, you can approach God with confidence and not with guilt and always worried that God is mad at you and ready to punish you when you do something wrong. If Christ took your guilt, it would be unfair for God to make you feel guilty for your sins.

> Therefore, there is now no condemnation for those who are in
> Christ Jesus.
> (Romans 8:1 KJV)

No condemnation means no condemnation. None! This destroys the formula that is playing out in most people's lives and emotions. There is no guilt, therefore there can be no condemnation. If there is no condemnation, there can be no shame. In fact, just as Jesus "bore" your sins, He also "bore" your shame on the cross.

> For in Scripture it says: "See, I lay a stone in Zion, a chosen and precious cornerstone, and the one who trusts in him will never be put to shame." (1Peter 2:6 NIV)

In the old covenant, they felt shame for their sin, and they felt tremendous remorse and emotional pain because of it. The new covenant says that if you trust in Jesus, you will **never** be put to shame. The word never means never! Ever! You will never, ever be put to shame for anything that you have done if you have placed your trust in Jesus. Which covenant do you want to live under? Most Christians are still living under the old covenant of shame.

I know. We still have a problem. None of us is capable of doing good.

Jesus Transferred His Goodness to Us

Goodness is a fruit of the Spirit. It is the opposite of guilt, shame, and condemnation. Because we are incapable of doing good, we needed Jesus to transfer His righteousness to us so we could be made right with God.

> God made him who had no sin to be sin for us, so that in him we might become the righteousness of God.
> (2 Corinthians 5:21 NIV)

This is what you need to believe to get rid of shame in your life: You are the righteousness of God in Christ. You are not righteous because you do good things or are a good person. You feel shame because without Christ you are not a good person. Our righteousness is filthy rags before God (Isaiah 64:6). Notice, that is old covenant language. Your righteousness is no longer filthy rags before God because you are now the righteousness of God in Christ. You have been made righteous because of Him.

That is new covenant thinking. When God sees you, He no longer sees your unrighteousness, He sees Christ's righteousness and therefore He has declared you righteous in Christ.

You have probably heard preachers say that you are a sinner saved by grace. That is not entirely true. You were a sinner saved by grace when you were saved. From that point on and for an eternity, you are now the righteousness of God in Christ. You are no longer a sinner, but you are made righteous in the sight of God.

Many, if not most, emotional problems will resolve themselves if you can grasp this truth. If you can see yourself as God sees you and you can accept that because Christ took your shame, you no longer have to take it upon yourself, then you can be set free from it.

When you feel shame, you can approach the throne of grace with confidence. There you will receive mercy and find grace to help you in your time of need. When you sin—and you will—you don't have to suffer the emotional consequences of those sins. You can go to the throne of God to receive mercy.

What Should Your Response be When You Sin?

Some men brought him a paralyzed man on a mat. When Jesus saw their faith, he said to the sick man, "Cheer up, son! For I have forgiven your sins!" (Matthew 9:2)

Jesus told the man to "cheer up!" The paralyzed man was depressed for obvious reasons. Jesus told him to rejoice because his sins were forgiven. He didn't say cheer up because He was about to heal him from his paralysis. He said to cheer up because his sins were forgiven.

The church tells us that we need to feel deep remorse for our sin. Do you remember the story of the girl at the beginning of the book, who got pregnant as a teenager? The church elders made her stand in front of the church and confess her sin openly to everyone. The purpose was to make her feel shame as if that somehow would incentivize her to never sin again.

Just the opposite happened. The shame caused her to believe she was a bad person. Because of that belief, even more sinful behavior followed. I recently learned that she is pregnant out of wedlock again with another man she is living with. Shame is the last thing we should want to make anyone feel for the sin.

For that matter, you are not to be depressed over your sins. You're not to feel deep regret and pain for years because you messed up. When you first sin, you should feel a conviction about the act. However, that should last as long as it takes for you to realize that your sins are forgiven through the blood of Christ.

So many of our prayers are wrong. We often pray and beg God to forgive us of our sins. Especially when something bad happens or we do something bad. We are feeling shame and often our instinct is to cry out to God to forgive us. He has already forgiven you! You don't have to ask Him to do something He has already done! Instead, you need to thank God for sending Jesus and thank Jesus for dying on the cross for your sins.

This is so freeing if you can get this concept. You don't have to live your life constantly feeling inadequate with God. You don't have to spend your life in constant guilt, condemnation, and shame, continually asking God to do something that He has already done.

Does that give everyone a license to sin? No. Just the opposite. When you realize that you are the righteousness of God in Christ, it makes you want to sin less. When you realize you're free from condemnation, you can live your life free from the power of sin over your life. If sin can no longer create shame in your life, and all your sin is already forgiven, you are free to live your life in the abundance that the provision intended.

Jesus told the woman caught in the act of adultery that He did not condemn her. Then He told her to go and sin no more (John 8). That's what Christ is telling us today. We're no longer condemned for our sin, even the horrible sin of adultery. We're set free from those sins, so go and sin no more, because you're not condemned, you are free from your sin.

This is a journey of faith. It's hard to believe God loved us so much that He gave His son to take away our guilt, condemnation, and shame, but He did. When my wife receives a rewards card from TJ Maxx, Ross, or Kohls, she gets really excited. I hope you are really excited about what Christ has done for you. Donna can't wait to get to the store to see what rewards await her. I hope that you can't wait to see what a life without guilt, condemnation, and shame feels like.

When you received Christ, you received a package deal. That package deal included freedom from sin, eternal life, and abundant life through Christ. The package deal included Christ bearing your sins and taking them upon Himself, but also Christ bearing your shame and

Let God Purify Your Conscience

Just think how much more the blood of Christ will purify our
consciences from sinful deeds so that we can worship the living God.
For by the power of the eternal Spirit, Christ offered himself to
God as a perfect sacrifice for our sins.
(Hebrews 9:14)

Your conscience is filled with the memory of your past sins and the
knowledge of the evil of those sins. For many people, the memory of
those sins keeps them bound to shame, depression, guilt, and a sense
of feeling worthless. The blood of Christ, however, was shed to
cleanse you of your sins and purify your conscience. You can stand
before God, whole, perfect and in right relationship with God and
self, knowing that Christ has set you free from the penalty or curse
of that sin!

The word *purify* means to sanitize or disinfect. It is like cleaning
your kitchen. You sanitize your counter to remove all the unwanted
germs and bacteria that can make you sick. God wants to completely sanitize your conscience from your past sins so that it
doesn't make you emotionally sick.

Then tap into the fruit of the Spirit, goodness, and you will have
the ability to go and sin no more.

14

Freedom from Fear

As human beings, we are limited to time and space. Our physical bodies can only live in the moment and in one location. We can't transport ourselves physically into the past or into the future. Emotions don't have the same limitations. With the help of memories, you can feel emotions today from things that happened years ago. With your imagination, you can travel into the future and feel emotions related to things that have not yet occurred and may never occur.

Generally, toxic emotions such as anger, bitterness, shame, and unforgiveness travel back in time, while anxiety and fear travel forward into an uncertain future. Unrestrained, these emotions give the enemy an open door to make your life miserable. Anytime he wants, he can play on your emotions by simply reminding you of a bad experience in your past or drawing on your worst fears and warning you that something bad is likely to happen in your future.

That's why it's important to limit your emotions to present reality. That way they're grounded in what is happening at that moment in time and not allowed free rein to roam through the recesses of your mind and cause you to feel conflicting emotions ruining your current reality.

Have you ever been really happy, doing something fun and having a good time when, all of a sudden, a memory comes into your mind and ruins the moment? Have you ever been at a birthday or

Christmas party and suddenly think about something coming up in the future that has you worried totally changing your mood?

Most of us have experienced those inopportune feelings one time or another and probably didn't know why. It's how Satan manipulates our emotions. This is where we get the term "push my buttons." Where do you think those buttons come from? They are toxic emotions established in the form of emotional roots that are just below the surface, and those emotions can be triggered at any time and for any reason without regard for what is happening in that moment.

We actually pay money to have our emotions manipulated. It's not hard for us to become emotionally attached to characters in movies and in books who don't exist. Producers and directors of films and television know that a movie will be boring if it doesn't invoke feelings in its audience. Therefore, every entertainment median has a heavy dose of mystery, suspense, excitement, and/or sadness.

It doesn't matter that the movies are unrealistic and irrational. The end goal is for the viewer to have an emotional experience that moves them in some way. Entire franchises are built around horror films designed to invoke intense feelings of fear. Sometimes the stimuli in horror films are so intense, they can cause nightmares and weird dreams. I still remember how scared I was watching Don Knotts in the *Ghost and Mister Chicken* as a child. Knowing what I know now and watching it as an adult, I realize how foolish it was to be so scared of a silly movie.

The Bible says to "fear not" 365 times. It's no surprise to me that the enemy wants you to feel fear at every opportunity. The purpose of the emotion of fear, if there really is a purpose, is to let you know you are in some kind of danger and a threat you need to be concerned about is nearby. In reality, there is nothing you are watching in a movie that is actually dangerous to you. That doesn't matter to the enemy. He wants you to experience fear as many times as possible until it is ingrained in your memory so he can bring fear to your recollection at any time.

The stimuli and demonic influence of those movies can be destructive to your emotional well-being. They teach you to feel fear when you don't need to. It reinforces in you a spirit of fear that Satan can control at any time. You need to avoid those kinds of movies and reject any spirit of fear that manifests in your life.

It is always important for emotions to be rooted in present reality and based on things actually happening in your life. One night several years ago, I had a bad dream. In that dream, my wife did something to make me really mad. The next morning, I woke up angry at her. Later that morning, I still wasn't over it. I told her about my dream and what I was feeling.

Her response was expected, "How can you be mad at me? I didn't do anything."

How foolish would it be for me to continue to be mad at her for something she didn't say or do in reality? That's how many people are with their emotions when they are lingering in the past or projecting into the future. Those feelings aren't based on reality no matter how strongly you feel them. When you express them or act upon them, then you play right into the enemy's hands.

Often, when I teach this principle, I get push back. I hear things like:

"I'm entitled to feel whatever I want."

"You have to accept me for who I am."

"I wear my emotions on my sleeve."

Wearing your emotions on your sleeves is not a good thing. Demanding that people accept your emotions, even if they are not based in reality, is profane. I have no right to be mad at my wife for something in my dream that she never did. You have no right to be angry at someone for something they did in the past that you were supposed to forgive them for and resolve on the same day that the offense occurred. You have no right to subject others to future worries and fears that are not based on present reality and may or may not ever happen.

Integrity insists that thoughts and emotions be grounded in truth. Present truth. Not memories and not prognostications. Once they are grounded in present truth, they can be processed through the filter of faithfulness which is the next fruit of the Spirit on our list.

Fear is the Opposite of Faith

What is fear? The Greek word for fear is *phobos*. That's where we get our word phobia. A phobia is an irrational fear of something. In the Greek, *phobos* means to withdraw or to flee. Even though the Bible tells us not to fear anything, on several occasions, the Bible tells us to flee temptation and the snares of the enemy. Right after Jesus was born, Joseph had a dream in which the Holy Spirit told him to take his family and flee to Egypt.

Herod was seeking to kill Jesus which would have destroyed all of God's redemptive plans for mankind. An angel warned Joseph and told him to flee the danger. Then he said to stay in Egypt until He told them it was safe to return. Some might say that Joseph acted out of fear. I would make a different argument. He acted out of faith. He trusted the direction of the Holy Spirit to keep him and his family safe.

If you are facing a dangerous situation, you don't need fear to protect you or tell you to flee. You have the Holy Spirit who leads you into all truth. Fear becomes an unnecessary emotion when you have the discernment and wisdom of the Holy Spirit working in your life.

The truth is that we have nothing to fear in this life because we can never be separated from the love of Christ:

> Who shall separate us from the love of Christ? Shall tribulation, or distress, or persecution, or famine, or nakedness, or danger, or sword? As it is written, "For your sake we are being killed all the day long; we are regarded as sheep to be slaughtered." No, in all these things we are more than conquerors through him who loved us. For I am sure that neither death nor life, nor angels nor rulers, nor things present nor things to come, nor powers, nor height nor depth, nor anything else in all creation, will be able to separate us from the love of God in Christ Jesus our Lord. (Romans 8:35-39 NKJV)

Unless we are separated from the love of Christ, we should not fear tribulation, distress, persecution, famine, nakedness, danger, or the sword. That covers just about anything you might be worried about in the future. The fact is that we have no fear because nothing can separate us from the love of God. With that assurance, there is nothing in your future to be afraid of.

The problem is, do you believe it? It is a fundamental question for every Christian to answer. Do you trust God to keep you safe?

I can hear the arguments from many as they are reading this because I've heard them when I have taught this.

"But bad things do happen."

"People can and do hurt us."

"There are many things in this world that are dangerous, and we should fear."

That's not what the Bible says. It says the only one we should fear is God.

And do not fear those who kill the body but cannot kill the soul. But rather fear Him who is able to destroy both soul and body in hell. (Matthew 10:28 NKJV)

The Bible calls it the "fear of the Lord." It's not fear in the way we think of fear. It's a reverence and worship of the Lord. It is the equivalent of the fruit of the Spirit, faithfulness, which is trusting, believing, and loyalty to God.

Fear, as a toxic emotion, is withdrawing and fleeing from your relationship with God. We think it is rational and normal to fear something dangerous to our mortal bodies. In reality, fear is not withdrawal from danger; it's withdrawal from your steadfast faithfulness to God. When you are afraid of something, it's because you don't trust God to deliver you from it.

I sought the Lord, and He heard me, And delivered me from
all my fears.
(Psalm 34:4 NKJV)

This lays out the formula to overcome fear. If there is something you are afraid of, you seek the Lord, and He will deliver you from all of your fears. Notice the word "all." That means every fear. You don't need to be afraid of anything in your present or in your future. You can trust God to protect you every step of the way.

There's an interesting story in the Bible about Elisha, a prophet of God and King Aram who was at war with Israel.[6] Every time Aram made a strategic battlefield maneuver, God told Elisha, who then warned the king of Israel. This enraged King Aram. He summoned his officers and demanded to know how the King of Israel was one step ahead of him every time. He believed that his officers must have been giving his battle plan secrets to the enemy.

One of the officers replied, "None of us have betrayed you. But Elisha, the prophet who is in Israel, tells the king of Israel the very words you speak in your bedroom."

The king ordered that Elisha be captured and brought to him. Of course, the king didn't know that God was with Elisha. He should've suspected, since Elisha's prophecies were so accurate. Nevertheless, the king's armies surrounded Elisha. They were determined to capture and kill him.

Elisha's servant woke him early in the morning and said, "Oh no, my Lord! What shall we do?"

Have you ever said those words or felt that level of fear? I know I have. Elisha calmly answered, "Don't be afraid. Those who are with us are more than those who are with them."

What happened next was nothing short of miraculous. Elisha prayed that his servant's eyes would be opened. When they were, the servant was able to see into the spiritual realm. The hills were full of a multitude of horses and chariots of fire all around Elisha, protecting them.

Elijah had nothing to fear. He prayed that God would strike the enemy with blindness, and God did exactly as Elisha had asked. Eventually, God gave them back their sight, but not before they had learned their lesson. The last verse in the chapter says, "So the bands from Aram stopped raiding Israel's territory."

I bet they did! Elisha and his servant didn't have to fear their enemies because God was protecting them. Elisha countered fear with faith. As New Testament believers, we can counter fear with the fruit of the Spirit, faithfulness. Faithfulness is a loyalty and trust in God and His protection for your life.

Fear Is Like Fortune-Telling

Saul died because he was unfaithful to the LORD; he did not keep
the word of the LORD and even consulted a medium for guidance.
(1 Chronicles 10:13 NKJV)

Saul was another king of Israel. If you study his life, you will find he
lived with a lot of fears. Most were justifiable in the natural. There
were a lot of people who sought to kill him. What you may not
know is that Saul actually took his own life. He was in the midst of
a battle and was so afraid he was going to be captured that he fell on
his own sword and committed suicide.

Saul didn't have to die. He was so afraid of his enemies. What he
should have been afraid of was his own toxic emotions of fear. He
didn't die at the hands of his enemies, he died because he did not
keep the Word of the Lord and consulted a medium for guidance. A
medium is a fortune-teller. It's someone who purports to be able to
see into the future and predicts what is going to happen. Saul went
to the medium for guidance. In other words, he wanted to know
what he could do to protect himself in the future from those who
sought to kill him.

Rather than going to God like Elisha did, Saul allowed his fears
to overwhelm him to the point that he turned away from God and
sought a sorcerer for comfort. That's what fear will do to you. It will
turn you away from trusting in God. The dictionary's definition of
fear is "an unpleasant emotion caused by the belief that someone or
something is dangerous, likely to cause pain, or a threat.

The threat may very well exist. It did for Elisha and for Saul. One
chose to ignore his fears and respond to his enemy with faith. The
other sought to compound his fears by seeking guidance from an
evil medium. Which one had the best outcome? The one who
trusted God.

That doesn't mean that your outcome will always be a good one. Sometimes bad things happen to good people. Your worst fears may come to pass. However, if you trust God and choose not to be afraid, then your response, by faith, opens the door for the miraculous to happen in your life.

It's important to realize that fear has no power. It's just a feeling. It can do nothing to you, other than make you feel uncomfortable. Fear is never from God. What is from God is power, love, and a sound mind. A sound mind means good judgment. A sound mind realizes that fear is unnecessary when there is no danger. Fear is only a feeling and has no power over you and you are actually the one with the power to make fear go away. Finally, a sound mind ultimately knows that there is nothing anyone on this earth can do to separate you from the love of God.

> There is no fear in love; but perfect love casts out fear, because
> fear involves torment. But he who fears has not been made
> perfect in love.
> (1 John 4:18 NKJV)

If you always know that God loves you, and that His love is perfect, you will never fear. Fear is torment to the soul. That word torment in the Greek can also mean punishment. Jesus came to free us from punishment. As a result, we are also free from fear.

15

Freedom from Pride

Emotions by definition are rooted in self-centeredness. An *emotion* is a state of feeling generally accompanied by physiological and behavioral changes in the body. Emotions are selfish feelings based on thoughts. That doesn't mean they are always a bad thing, it just means that your emotions are most interested in you and physiological and behavioral changes are present to get you to pay attention to them. I believe those physiological and behavioral changes are often enhanced and intensified by the enemy to get you to act on them.

Consequently, feelings should not be trusted no matter how intense they may seem. The feelings should be run through the filter of God's Word to determine if they line up with what you should be feeling if walking in the spirit rather than the flesh. If they don't, they should be rejected out of hand and ignored. Further, if they are not based in present reality, they should be compartmentalized and moved out of the mainstream of your thoughts.

Not that thoughts are any better. The Bible says that there is a way that seems right to a man, but its end is the way of death.¹ I hope I haven't given you the wrong impression. I am not purporting that you should walk around like a mind-numbed robot never feeling anything and totally relying on your thoughts. Toxic thoughts can lead to destruction just as quickly as toxic emotions. Some of the most brilliant minds in the world are atheists. Their thoughts have led them to the tragic and false conclusion that there is no God.

The point is that thoughts and feelings go hand-in-hand and can lead to trouble in your life. That's because the root of toxic emotions and negative thoughts is pride. Pride is confidence in yourself. We often make the mistake of thinking that pride is simply arrogance. That's part of it for sure, but pride is much more than that. It is a self-centeredness that leads to self-reliance which, when it results in rebellion against God and His ways, leads to sin.

Over the last few chapters, I have shown you how toxic emotions are directly opposite of the fruit of the Spirit in how they affect your moods and your actions. Notice the selfish thoughts that accompany toxic emotions:

Lust	I want that.
Depression	Woe is me.
Anxiety	I'm worried.
Discontentment	I deserve Better.
Anger	You hurt me.
Shame	I'm a bad person.
Fear	I'm in danger
Price	I'm better than you are

These emotions are all me-centered and are almost always based on wrong thoughts. Those thoughts and emotions cause you to put your confidence in yourself rather than in God which is the essence of pride.

The wicked in his proud countenance does not seek God; God is in
none of his thoughts.
(Psalm 10:4 NKJV)

Pride causes man to conclude there is no God or that he doesn't
need God. Pride, as a toxic emotion, leads a person to become
haughty, arrogant, and have a misplaced sense of worth. It leads to a
judgmental and divisive nature, creating conflict with those who
you perceive as inferior to your way of thinking or your feelings.

Pride causes you to lash out in anger when others don't validate
your feelings or thoughts. Sin is the disregarding of God's will for
your life. When you face a temptation, pride is what leads you to
choose sin over the narrow path. It is the selfish decision that you
want what you want no matter how much it hurts you or those
around you.

Pride is in Opposition to God

God opposes the proud, but gives grace to the humble.
(James 4:6)

Gentleness is the opposite of pride and is the next fruit of the Spirit
on our list. Gentleness is defined as meekness and humility. God actually opposes the proud and works against them, but His favor is
on those who are humble. Do you want God working for you or
against you? He is always for you and wants what is best for you but
won't let your pride go unopposed.

When you sin, you will face resistance at every turn. You may not
realize it, but there will be forces at work to expose the sin and
bring it to light. Pride and sin bring tremendous pain and suffering
once the destruction comes and the sin is exposed. Pride thinks you
will avoid those consequences. It argues that no one will ever find
out your secrets.

God knows your innermost feelings and thoughts. He will never be fooled. Not that He's standing by waiting to pounce on your pride. His opposition is for your benefit. He knows the heartache that awaits you if you continue in your own self-reliance and try to exclude Him from consideration. It's impossible for us to fully understand how much God hates pride. In the list of things God hates, pride is the first one mentioned. It's understandable why that is true. Pride is confidence in yourself. It says to God that you don't need Him and that you can handle your circumstances and troubles on your own.

If you don't already realize it, you should now: You have nothing apart from God. He could end your existence at any moment of His choosing. Every breath you take comes from Him. Every morsel of food that you put in your mouth comes from God's provision. We are literally nothing but dust if not for Him. Fortunately, He is a good God and none of us gets what we deserve because of His grace. But that's why He hates pride so much. It is foolish for us to say we know better than God or that we are going to go against God's will for our lives no matter the consequences. It is the essence of pride.

Pride rejects your reliance on God and looks to yourself for survival. To my knowledge, pride has never added one second to a person's life or has allowed anyone to escape the consequences of rebelling against God. The only escape from those consequences is grace. God gives grace to the humble. The only conclusion one should reach is that rejecting pride and recognizing your reliance on God is the best way to live.

Do you see how emotions are rooted in pride? If you feel fear, your natural reaction is to deal with the danger yourself. If you are anxious, you lack confidence in God to be able to handle whatever you are worried about. If you are depressed, then you are saying to God that you don't believe He will work all things together for your good. When those toxic feelings are compared to Scripture, the choice becomes clear; do you believe in God and His Word or do you put more trust in your feelings?

> For the Lord will be your confidence, And will keep your
> foot from being caught.
> (Proverbs 3:26 NKJV)

When your confidence is in the Lord, He gives you grace to face your circumstances and troubles and will keep your foot from being caught. If you reject His help and rely on your own feelings and thoughts, the path will lead to destruction.

> For the flesh lusts against the Spirit, and the Spirit against the flesh;
> and these are contrary to one another, so that you do not do the
> things that you wish.
> (Galatians 5:17 NKJV)

This is a powerful verse that will help you understand what is happening inside of you. Your toxic feelings and negative thoughts are actually at war with the Spirit. Pride is at war with gentleness. Fear is at war with faith. Anxiety is at war with peace. They are contrary to each other. The Spirit of God living inside you is fighting against your feelings to try and keep you from doing the things that you wish to do. Why? The Spirit knows that if you do what you want, the path will eventually lead to destruction.

Why does a parent restrain a child who is about to walk in the road without looking both ways? To keep that child from harming himself. We are all children of God. He opposes our pride to protect us from harm.

> Pride goes before destruction, And a haughty spirit before a fall.
> (Proverbs 16:18 NKJV)

The Greek word for *haughty* means to blow smoke. It paints a picture of being puffed up or high minded. I see it as rationalization. Pride is a feeling or thought that you are right, and others are wrong. Perhaps even God is wrong. When sin is rationalized, you become convinced that you can sin without the consequences.

Look at Judas, the disciple who denied Christ for thirty pieces of silver. He walked with Jesus every day for three years. When Jesus healed the blind man, Judas was there. He witnessed every miracle and teaching of Jesus. Even so, Judas's love of money and his pride caused him to fall into temptation.

We don't know all of what he was thinking, but it's not hard to imagine. He may have thought that there was no way Jesus would die even if Judas turned him into the authorities. Jesus had raised Lazarus from the dead. Surely, there was nothing the Romans or Pharisees could do to Jesus. That might have factored into Judas's thinking.

Judas may have been sinning for a while. He was in charge of overseeing Jesus's money. The Bible doesn't say, but I wouldn't be surprised to learn that he had pilfered money from the treasury all along seemingly without getting caught and with no consequences. That would have given him confidence that he could get away with betraying Jesus. That was a confidence in himself and not in God.

Once he realized his dreadful mistake, and Jesus was being led to his death, Judas was in such remorse that he gave the money back and went out and hanged himself. That is a perfect example of pride coming before the fall. When you live your life based on feelings, eventually those feelings will betray you. Your feelings and thoughts will never be a hundred percent right, all the time. They will lead you astray. Eventually, they will lead to a fall.

So many people make decisions every day based on their feelings. The Bible says they are like a reed tossed in the wind.[7] Whichever way the wind blows is how they feel. God is the same yesterday, to-day, and forever. His Word never changes. He never lies or changes the rules on you in midstream. You can always count on Him to be faithful. Can you honestly say that the same is true for your feelings and thoughts? Can you honestly say that your feelings have never led you astray? Everyone reading this book can remember a time when they made a wrong decision based on their feelings and thoughts.

Consequences of the Fall

When pride leads to self-reliance, then it generally leads to rejection of God's will for your life. That is your emotions deceiving you and leading to you to believe that what you think or feel is right. That leads to a fall, which leads to disgrace. The fall only leads to more toxic emotions.

Disappointment

Disappointment is a sadness over unmet expectations. When expectations are rooted in pride, then when they don't come to pass, the natural response is disappointment in God, yourself, and/or others. Pride led you to believe that you deserved a good outcome. When you didn't get it, then you retreated back into more self-centeredness and looked for someone to blame.

When you trust in the Lord, you will not be disappointed. Does that mean everything always worked out the way that you wanted it to? No. You will have trouble in this world. However, if your reliance is in the Lord with humility, everything will always work together for your good even if you don't see it at the time.

Regret

Regret is sadness over a mistake you made that caused you or someone else pain. This feeling is a consequence of the fall that came from pride. Someone once said that sin will take you farther than you want to go, keep you longer than you want to stay, and cost you more than you want to pay.[10] That is something to keep in mind before you let your pride lead you into sin.

Pride insists that the above statement is not true. It deceives you into believing that you can hide your sin from others and from God. In some cases, pride causes many to flaunt their sins and openly rebel against God. They are absolutely astounded when that pride leads to destruction.

Some are using the grace message to justify sinning. "I live under grace, so it doesn't matter what I do." Paul dealt with that in Galatians and said it was foolish thinking. While we do live under grace and all our sins are forgiven, we still have to face consequences on this earth for our sins. Part of the consequences is living with toxic emotions. Grace came to free you from the toxic emotions. That doesn't mean you can sin all you want and just keep coming back for more grace. If you do, you are in for a life filled with a lot of heartache.

Don't take my word for it. Look up the suicide rate for people who engage in behaviors contrary to the Word of God. It is through the roof. Find data on the percentage of people who divorce who eventually regret it. Ninety-seven percent of relationships that start in an affair fail. It feels so good at first. If it's so good, why does it lead such a path of destruction behind it. That is proof positive that the feelings and thoughts that deceive people into those behaviors ultimately leads to a fall and a life filled with regrets.

We've all done things in the past we regret.

For godly grief produces a repentance that leads to salvation without regret, whereas worldly grief produces death.
(2 Corinthians 7:10 ESV)

We've all done things in the past we regret. There is such a thing as "godly grief." It is the realization that your pride has led you to sin against God. That grief leads to repentance and a resolve to not fall into that sin again. Salvation takes away the regret. Worldly grief is regret that doesn't lead to repentance. It eventually produces death. If you ever want to really feel free from your emotions, you have to allow the godly grief that comes from sin to lead you to repentance and a resolve to sin no more.

Insecurity

Insecurity manifests in a number of questions:

What will others think of me?

What will people say?

What if I fail?

What if I'm not right?

Insecurity is a future worry rooted in pride. It's a lack of confidence in yourself, but also a lack of confidence in God. It is a natural feeling that comes with pride. Insecurity is the uneasy feeling that you have stepped out of God's will and onto a path of possible destruction. Pride is a mask for insecurity.

In the midst of this global pandemic, our state has had a mask mandate for more than six months. The mask is supposed to cover your mouth and nose and protect you from the virus. In a similar way, people wear emotional masks thinking it will protect their feelings. The outward manifestation is generally pride or false humility meant to cover up the hidden insecurities behind the facade.

The behavioral masks are things like self-deprecation. To mask insecurities, people will go around pretending to be humble. That is a form of pride and self-centeredness in and of itself. Some use humor to keep people at arms-length. They are always joking and making fun of circumstances or themselves. Some are continually putting on a happy face so that no one can see that they are dying inside. While others may not be able to see behind the masks, the toxic emotions are there anyway.

Egotism and self-promotion are meant to portray a false picture of success when the person is afraid of others seeing their real condition. So many times, in marriage counseling, one or both of the spouses are shocked at the behavior of their spouse when they learned about it. In our society, we have become good at hiding our real emotions and masking them in pride. Because pride comes before the fall, eventually toxic emotions surface, the mask is removed, and the person is exposed. The seemingly perfect life crumbles like a house of cards.

It generally takes a fall for that to happen. When it does, the person and everyone around him or her is left devastated. Thankfully, we have the grace of God that restores everyone who repents and receives forgiveness from God. Hopefully, the offended extends grace as well so there can be restoration. More often than not, when a person falls, they are met with judgment and hatred. Hatred is another manifestation of pride.

Hatred

Hatred is an emotion that God feels. However, God only hates things that are evil. He doesn't hate people, and He wants you to limit your feelings of hate to things that are unholy and unrighteous. You can hate injustice. You can hate prejudice, racism, lying, divorce, war, and conflict and all manners of evil, but your feelings of hatred should never be directed toward another person.

There are six things the Lord hates, seven that are detestable to him: haughty eyes, a lying tongue, hands that shed innocent blood, a heart that devises wicked schemes, feet that are quick to rush into evil, a false witness who pours out lies and a person who stirs up conflict in the community. (Proverbs 6:16-19 NIV)

Notice how pride is the very first thing listed. God hates pride, and it is detestable to him. This is a revealing list of the kinds of things God hates. You should limit your feelings of hate to the same type of things. Hatred becomes a toxic emotion when it is directed toward people. When you hate someone, you allow the emotion of hate to become potentially destructive to that person and to the relationship. You may hate the evil someone does, but you are not to hate the person, even an evil and unrighteous person.

Pride leads to judging others and can even lead to hatred when someone doesn't meet your expectations. The Bible says that those feelings are foolish.

For we ourselves were also once foolish, disobedient, deceived, serving various lusts and pleasures, living in malice and envy, hateful and hating one another. (Titus 3:3 NKJV)

I don't wish to sound insensitive. Feelings seem real, and they are sometimes strong. The purpose of this book is to show you that those feelings are foolish. Toxic emotions are what you used to feel before you were saved. Now that you are a new creation, you are no longer enslaved to various lusts and pleasures. You don't need to spend your life in malice, envy, pride, and hating one another.

There is a better way to live: Feeling free from those past emotions.

16

Freedom from Addictions

Do not let sin control the way you live; do not give in to
sinful desires.
(Romans 6:12)

Addictions, by definition, are not based in present reality. They are
rooted in past emotions and sustained by artificial rewards. The
definition of *addiction* is a compulsive search or need for physical or
emotional escape through habit-forming substances that supply
short-term, psychological relief of deeper-rooted pain.

An addict is defined as one inclined to indulge in something re-
peatedly. Another definition is one who has a compulsive, obsessive,
or psychological need to engage in a behavior or activity that is
habit forming. In other words, you can't be considered addicted
without considering past behaviors and accumulating them into an
arbitrary number that crosses a line into what some might consider
an addiction.

The problem with that is that God's mercies are new every morning. Every day we wake up with a new opportunity to serve God and
break free from past behaviors and future worries. God even has the
uncanny ability to not remember our sins anymore. He doesn't ac-
cumulate them into a ledger that proves you have indulged in a behavior too many times in the past, therefore, you are bound to them
today and in the future.

This book rejects the idea that your present peace is determined
by past circumstances. Instead, every day you can release the past so

178

the pain of those memories can be overcome by the power of the Holy Spirit without chemically or artificially numbing your senses. The Bible is full of verses that support the mandate that God can redeem a person's past at any moment, cleansing him from all unrighteousness, breaking every chain or bondage, and redeeming the time by transforming even the worst sinner in the blink of an eye.

That is not to say that addictions aren't real. The Latin root of the word "addict" means to give over or surrender to. That is a much better description of an addiction. It is a surrendering of your will to the control of something or someone else, namely sinful desires. It is as Romans 6:12 says, "letting sin control the way you live."

A person is not an addict today because they engaged in the behavior in the past. They are an addict today if they give over and surrender their will today. In the same way, invoking the power of the fruit of the Spirit, namely self-control, the person can be free at any time and choose to surrender his will to the power of the Holy Spirit and not the addictive substance or behavior.

That is an exciting truth. You can choose at any moment in time to surrender your life to the Holy Spirit and change the direction of your life. Of course, you can also continue to surrender to the lusts of your flesh and the worldly emotions that have held you captive for so long. Make no mistake. It is a daily choice.

Many "addicts" choose freedom one day, only to surrender it again to the addiction the next. For instance, most people who smoke have quit many times. They intuitively know it's bad for them, so they try to quit in their own self-control. If they quit, even for a short period of time, they have proven the power of choice. Even if for a moment, they showed control over the so-called addiction and stepped out of the past into a new present reality.

An alcoholic may only drink on the weekends. That is evidence of some self-control. A drug abuser can go months without drugs in a controlled rehab center. The idea that you cannot control your addiction is a myth. Every addict exercises some level of control over his addiction. The problem is that most people don't realize that their self-control is not as powerful to break the behavior as the self-control provided by the Holy Spirit.

You Can Control Your Behaviors

You can control your behaviors, but usually it's only temporarily.

I counseled a man with an anger problem. He would get extremely angry at his wife to the point of being verbally and almost physically abusive. He made the statement that he can't control his anger.

I asked him, "When a police officer pulls you over and gives you a ticket, do you scream and yell at him?"

"Of course not," the guy responded. "I don't want to go to jail!"

"When you are at work and your boss makes you mad, do you yell and scream and threaten to hit him?"

He replied, "No. I would never do that."

"Why not?"

"I don't want to get fired!" he said incredulously.

I pointed out the obvious to him. "You can control your anger in certain circumstances. You control your anger when you want to control it. The issue is not that you can't control your anger; the question is why don't you control it with your wife?"

While it may be true that a Christian may struggle with relinquishing control of his emotions and body to his sinful desires, it is not an unconditional surrender. Every believer has been bought with a price. We cannot even give total control over to our sinful desires. Our destinies have already been determined by the provision of Christ on the cross.

That being said, the Bible is clear that man has a free-will, so we have the power to momentarily choose surrender. However, it is short-term, even if it is repetitive. This is why God gave us the Holy Spirit. In our own strength, we are weak and tend to fall prey to our flesh-driven desires, cravings, and emotions.

That's why most diets fail, most smokers can't quit, and most alcoholics fall off the wagon over and over again. They're trying to change their behaviors in their own strength. In a way, they're trying to be their own god.

There is a better way. When empowered by the Holy Spirit, we have a supernatural ability to surrender to His strength and will for our lives.

> The temptations in your life are no different from what others experience. And God is faithful. He will not allow the temptation to be more than you can stand. When you are tempted, he will show you a way out so that you can endure. (1 Corinthians 10:13)

This verse could not be clearer. God does not allow anyone to be tempted beyond what he can stand. Therefore, the idea that a person cannot control an addiction is contrary to God's Word. God will never allow the present moment temptation to be more than what a person can overcome. While He is giving you the strength to overcome the addiction, He also promises to show you a way out. There is always a way out of an addiction. You always have the freedom to choose to let God help you. In fact, one of the major causes of addictive behavior is too much freedom.

> For you have been called to live in freedom, my brothers and sisters. But don't use your freedom to satisfy your sinful nature. Instead, use your freedom to serve one another in love. (Galatians 5:13)

God created us with the freedom to make choices. At any given time, we can choose good or evil. Christ set us free from the law of sin and death. However, you can become so free in your behavior that you become a slave to the behavior. The above verse clearly states that man has a choice. He can use his freedom to satisfy his sinful nature or he can use his freedom to serve another person. At any given point in time, anyone can choose to surrender to an activity, or he can choose not to indulge in the harmful activity and serve another person.

This is a powerful verse of truth. An addiction is based on self-centeredness. It's based on selfish behaviors. Satisfying your sinful nature is putting your own desires above everything else, including God's will for your life. Turning your focus from yourself to serving others, frees you from surrendering your will to your desires. If your focus is on serving God, you have no opportunity to serve yourself.

This is empowering. Many people lose hope because they think they are helpless to overcome the addiction. That is exactly what the enemy wants you to think. He wants you to think that you are such a bad person you will never get over the addiction. He wants to put a label on it, medicate it, and have you believe that you must "own it" and then convince you to wear the label of it for the rest of your life.

He wants you to become identified with your addiction. I want you to become identified as a servant of Christ. One of the best ways to overcome an addiction is to ask God where you might volunteer to serve others and be the source of hope, help, and healing they need. That takes your focus off yourself and on to serving others the way God has asked us to serve.

Past Behaviors Don't Define Your Present Identity in Christ

I was counseling a man who made the statement, "I'm an alcoholic." He said that, even though he hadn't had a drink in seven years. Remember the teaching in a previous chapter? Beliefs turn into thoughts; thoughts turn into feelings; feelings turn into actions. He believed that he was an alcoholic, and he had been told that "once an alcoholic, always an alcoholic." He believed the lie, and the belief was causing him emotional pain. The actual sin of drunkenness was not the problem; the label and the belief were the problem. Instead of living in freedom through Christ, he was still partnered with the lie of the enemy.

He struggled with the thoughts: "I'm a bad person, I can't control my behaviors, I'm damaged goods. No one is going to love me because I am an alcoholic. God doesn't love me because I am too bad a sinner." Consequently, he felt the emotions of insecurity, loneliness, guilt, shame, condemnation, fear, anxiety, depression, and regret. In addition, because he believed he was an alcoholic, he was under the risk of falling back into those behaviors because we eventually live out our identities. We become who we believe we are.

I told him, "You're not an alcoholic. You're the righteousness of God in Christ. Don't let your past behavior define your present reality. You haven't had a drink in years. Believe who you are today; redeemed, transformed, changed, an overcomer, and a child of God."

He played baseball in college. I asked him if he was still a college baseball player. He acknowledged that he wasn't.

"Why not?" I asked him.

"I haven't played baseball in fifteen years," he replied.

"That's my point. You haven't had a drink in seven years. You are not an alcoholic."

If you have ever suffered through an addiction and you have overcome it, then your identity should be in the mercy of God who has redeemed you from those addictions. Get rid of the labels given to you by the enemy. Don't let the curse of the enemy become your nickname. Get rid of the stigma. Don't allow the world to label you an alcoholic, a drug addict, a prostitute, an adulterer, or any other label the world wants to place on your past behavior.

If you have been set free from your past, then rejoice in it and wear the cross of Christ proudly. You are now the righteousness of God in Christ. By the way, that is an eternal truth. Alcoholism, drug abuse, fornication, adultery, pornography, and every addiction are temporary. They will eventually pass away. Why are we using temporary labels and not embracing the permanent, eternal label that God has placed on us?

Even if you are drinking or indulging in an addictive behavior today, it still is not your eternal identity. If you focus more on your eternal identity, it will shift your focus off the addiction and on to who you are in Christ.

Don't Let the Enemy make Your Sins Cumulative

So, what does someone do if he has not yet been set free from the so-called "addictions?" This section is for those people. If you are still struggling with addictions, then the same mercy that instantly redeemed Paul is available to you today in this very moment. God wants to set you free today of whatever it is that you have surrendered your will to. Your first step is to accept God's forgiveness for any past, present, or future sins:

The problem with the definition of addiction is that it makes sin cumulative. It ties your present reality to your past decisions and assumes you will do the behaviors today because you did them in the past. It leads to a belief that you can't change your present reality because you couldn't change your behavior in the past. It is basically saying you are too weak to overcome your weaknesses. While that may be true in your own strength, I reject that concept. I believe that Christ in you is the hope of your salvation, and He gives you all the strength you need to overcome. The key is in really believing that truth.

Even if you did the behavior yesterday, it's still in your past, and doesn't mean you have to do it today. While past behavior can be a predictor of future behavior, it's not definitive when it comes to God who can intervene in a person's life at any time. The Bible says that God is always ever present to help you now with whatever you need regardless of your past.

God doesn't keep a record of wrongs, so He's no longer looking at your sin as cumulative. When Christ was on the cross, the sins of the entire world were placed upon Jesus. At that moment, sins were cumulative. That's the only time in history where that happened. Since the cross, God is not looking at your sin; He is looking at the provision of Christ who has freed you of all sins. You have already been set free by Christ. You live "set free" the moment you realize you are already free.

That is true even when you are engaging in sinful behavior. You are still the righteousness of God. That doesn't change just because you are indulging in your flesh. If fact, it is during those times that you can be most aware of it. The problem is that we too often forget it.

A dog was chained to a pole in the back yard for several years. The chain allowed him to move ten yards in any direction. Over time, the dog accepted his limitations. One day, the chain came free from the pole but was still around the dog's neck. The dog stayed within the ten-yard radius even though he was no longer bound to the pole. He didn't know he was free because the chain was still around his neck.

If you are in Christ, you have already been set free from whatever you have surrendered your will to, even if it is a sinful behavior. However, the chain might still be around your neck. That's the problem with how we view addictions. They are cemented into your past and memory, and there's an expectation that they are so strong that they are going to take a long time to get over if you can even get over them. That is contrary to the Word of God. The Bible says that God can do anything now. The Bible uses the word "now" more than 2,500 times!

> For God says, "At just the right time, I heard you. On the day of salvation, I helped you." Indeed, the "right time" is now. Today is the day of salvation. (2 Corinthians 6:2)

God said that at the right time He would hear you and help you. Then He defines the right time as now! Today is the day of salvation. That is present reality. If not now, when? You don't have to live one more day surrendering your will to an addiction. You can be set free immediately by surrendering your will to the Holy Spirit.

You Are Set Free by the Holy Spirit

So I say, walk by the Spirit, and you will not gratify the desires of the flesh.
(Galatians 5:16 NIV)

The terms "walk by the Spirit" simply means to allow the Holy Spirit to control your flesh. As we have seen, an addiction is allowing the sin to control your flesh. If you allow the power of the Holy Spirit to control your flesh with the fruit of the Spirit of self-control, you will not carry out the desires of the flesh, and the addiction will be broken for as long as the Spirit is controlling your desires. The Greek word for self-control means self-dominion. Webster's Dictionary defines it as the ability to control your emotions or actions. For our purposes, I would define it as the supernatural ability to control your emotions or actions.

> I pray that God, the source of hope, will fill you completely with joy and peace because you trust in him. Then you will overflow with confident hope through the power of the Holy Spirit. I am fully convinced, my dear brothers and sisters, that you are full of goodness. (Romans 15:13-14)

That is the work of the Holy Spirit in your life. When the Holy Spirit controls your flesh, then you are filled completely with joy and peace, and confident hope will overflow inside of you. Notice the word, "completely." When you are filled with the Spirit, there is no room for anything but joy and peace. There is no room for anxiety or depression. There is no room in your flesh for fear or anger. The Spirit of God completely fills your flesh and controls all your emotions and your sinful desires. Addiction is not possible at that point because the Spirit of God is stronger and more powerful than your compulsion to engage in a certain behavior. Then you are free.

Alcoholics are told to keep track of how many days they have been sober. I'm sure you've heard someone say something like, "I haven't had a drink in seven years, two months, and nine days." In this book, I want to give people a new reality. If you are in Christ, you have been free for more than two thousand years!

17

Enter the Rest

"Do I have to go to church today?" I asked my dad when I was a young boy.

He replied, "No. You don't *have* to go to church. You *get* to go to church today."

I'll always remember my dad saying that, and it's a principle I've applied to a number of areas of my life. As it relates to emotions, it's certainly true. You don't *have* to be free from your emotions, you *get* to be.

I realize that statement may seem counterintuitive and unrealistic. That's because we have accepted toxic emotions as "normal" in our society and in many cases surrendered our wills to them. This book says you don't have to. I know. Living in present reality is a radical concept. It goes against everything the world teaches about emotions. But the Bible implores Christians to be different from the world.

The truth is that you will have trouble in this world. With trouble comes emotional pain. I don't deny that. Neither does the Bible. What I hope that I have convinced you to see is that Jesus made a provision for your emotional pain. That provision is rest.

I am leaving you with a gift—peace of mind and heart. And the peace I give is a gift the world cannot give. So don't be troubled or afraid. (John 14:27)

Jesus spoke those words to His disciples shortly before He went to His death and then left this world. He said that, after He was gone, they might be troubled or afraid. So, He left them a gift: peace of mind and heart. Then Jesus clarified that the world could not give it to them.

Please understand that. You cannot find peace in this world. You can't find happiness in indulging your flesh and living in your toxic emotions. For that matter, secular counselors, medications, drugs, alcohol, sex, money, relationships, etc., can't give you the peace I'm talking about. That only comes from God. Notice that Jesus said it was a gift. It's a free gift of grace.

> So there is a special rest still waiting for the people of God. For all who have entered into God's rest have rested from their labors, just as God did after creating the world. So let us do our best to enter that rest. (Hebrews 4:9-11)

That special rest is freedom from negative emotions. You can experience the fruit of the Spirit anywhere and anytime because He lives inside you. Because it's a free gift; it's not something you have to earn. You don't have to become a better person to enter into the rest. You don't have to be free from sin to experience the rest. You just have to believe God and choose to enter into the rest. There you will find total peace.

The word *unrest* means a disturbed or uneasy state. In my forty plus years of counseling, I've seen thousands of people in a disturbed or uneasy state. I've felt the same way myself many times. This book is not some ethereal theological exercise. It deals with real life and real pain and heartache. It's written because I have so much compassion for people in pain. Especially when the pain is unnecessary and there is a provision for it. How do you access that provision?

The King James version of the Bible says it this way: *Let us labour therefore to enter into that rest...*
(Hebrews 4:11)

That captures the struggle. It's something you will have to work at. That sounds like a contradiction in terms: "Work to rest." The reason it rings true is because it's not something that will come naturally to you. It requires denying the flesh and all of its powers. The great thing about rest is that God will help you enter into it. Just a couple of verses later in that same chapter, the Bible tells you what to do when you need help entering into rest.

Let us therefore come boldly to the throne of grace, that we may obtain mercy and find grace to help in time of need.
(Hebrews 4:16 KJV)

Rest is something you must seize. This verse says you obtain mercy, and you find grace when you are in a time of need. Where do you obtain and find them? At the throne of grace. You bring your requests to God, believe by faith that He will help you, and leave with peace and rest.

Jesus Said He Would Help You

Come to Me, all you who labor and are heavy laden, and I will give you rest. Take My yoke upon you and learn from Me, for I am gentle and lowly in heart, and you will find rest for your souls. (Matthew 11:28-29 NKJV)

Isn't it exciting to know that Christ has made a provision for every trouble that you will ever face? That should bring you great comfort and great joy just from reading that verse. That is the gospel of grace. The word *gospel* means good news. Gospel actually means news that is too good to be true. While the gospel is not too good to be true, it just seems that way.

You don't have to grieve the loss of a loved one and your sorrows only last for a night. That sounds too good to be true. You don't have to worry or be anxious about anything, because God said He would never leave you nor forsake you. It sounds too good to be true, but it's not. It is true. You can count on it.

However, you must come to Him to receive it. If you will turn to Christ, you will find rest for your soul. Jesus said to come to Him when you are emotional (heavy laden.) Come to Jesus and you will find rest. It doesn't say come to Jesus and He will solve your problems. It just says that He will give you rest in the midst of them. The challenge of overcoming emotions is to enter into the rest no matter how difficult your circumstances.

Don't Fall Short of It

Therefore, since a promise remains of entering His rest, let us fear lest any of you seem to have come short of it. For indeed the gospel was preached to us as well as to them; but the word which they heard did not profit them, not being mixed with faith in those who heard it. For we who have believed do enter that rest, as He has said: "So I swore in My wrath, 'They shall not enter My rest,'" (Hebrews 4:1-3 NKJV)

This is a sobering reality. The peace of God and His Word will not profit you if you don't believe it by faith. Only those who believe enter that rest. The last part of the verse is referring to the children of Israel who wandered in the desert for forty years because they would not enter into God's rest even after He had delivered them from slavery in Egypt.

Do you remember the story from the book of Exodus? They had been slaves in Egypt for more than 400 years. They cried out to God with sorrow and groanings. Imagine how much emotional pain and physical pain they were in while living as slaves to Pharaoh. God said that He had "seen their sorrows." They were living a life of sorrows.

God heard their cries and sent Moses to deliver them. The problem was that things got worse before they could get better. Pharaoh took away their straw for making bricks. That created a tremendous burden for them. Things were so bad, the leaders went and, "cried out to Pharaoh." Rather than trusting God, they became more emotionally unstable. Even to the point of begging Pharaoh to go easier on them.

Rather than turning to God and trusting in Him, they actually turned to their taskmaster to make their circumstances better. They had so much hope when Moses came on the scene, but when their circumstances got worse, their faith failed them. So much so that the children of Israel were murmuring and complaining and crying for Moses to leave.

Then the ten plagues came on Egypt. Water turned to blood. It says the river stank. Frogs invaded every house, bedroom, and kneading bowl. The whole land was littered with dead frogs. Lice came on every man and beast, and flies were so prevalent that the entire land was corrupted. All of the livestock was diseased, and darkness came over the entire earth. Even then, Pharaoh still would not let them go.

The final plague was the worst. Every firstborn child was to be killed. Imagine how you would feel if you were living that night. As difficult as circumstances are in your life, they could not be any worse than what they were facing.

Then Moses said, "Thus says the Lord: 'About midnight I will go out into the midst of Egypt; and all the firstborn in the land of Egypt shall die, from the firstborn of Pharaoh who sits on his throne, even to the firstborn of the female servant who is behind the handmill, and all the firstborn of the animals. Then there shall be a great cry throughout all the land of Egypt, such as was not like it before, nor shall be like it again. (Exodus 11:4-6 NKJV)

The cry was the worst mankind had ever seen or would ever see. The suffering was as bad as it could possibly be. The only thing they had to go on was that God promised they would be protected.

For the Lord will pass through to strike the Egyptians; and when He sees the blood on the lintel and on the two doorposts, the Lord will pass over the door and not allow the destroyer to come into your houses to strike you. (Exodus 12:23 NKJV)

God said that He would protect them from the plague. They didn't know if He would or not. They just had to trust Him. I can imagine there were many who were anxious and worried all night long, wondering if the blood on the doorpost would actually save them. With the ability of hindsight, do you know what they should have done? They could do nothing about their circumstances. They had already done what God told them to do and put the blood on the post. Once they did that, they just needed to go to sleep.

When they woke up the next morning, God had saved them. They plundered the Egyptians and left on a journey to the Promised Land. However, their troubles didn't end. They needed food and water and had to rely on God to provide it for them. They came upon the Red Sea and Pharaoh's army was bearing down on them. If God hadn't parted the waters, they would have been brought back to slavery.

This is an important lesson to learn: you will need God again and again to provide you with rest. Once one trouble is over, another is just around the corner. You will have to labor again and again to maintain that free gift of rest. The children of Israel were unable to do it.

> For who, having heard, rebelled? Indeed, was it not all who came out of Egypt, led by Moses? Now with whom was He angry forty years? Was it not with those who sinned, whose corpses fell in the wilderness? And to whom did He swear that they would not enter His rest, but to those who did not obey? So we see that they could not enter in because of unbelief. (Hebrews 3:16-19 NKJV)

They would not enter His rest. He wanted them to rest in His word and not worry but because of their unbelief they continued to struggle with their emotions. Exodus 16: 2-3 says that the children of Israel grumbled before Moses and said they wished they had just died in Egypt.

Their faith was tested, and they failed. That's how faith works. It's tested again and again. The enemy will always try and steal your peace. He's not going to let you enter into the rest without making you work for it. You'll be tempted to let your emotions get the best of you. The sooner you can reject the toxic emotions, mix them with faith, and enter into rest, the sooner you will feel free from them.

As He is, so are We in This World

When the Lord Jesus had finished talking with them, he was taken up into heaven and sat down in the place of honor at God's right hand. (Mark 16:19)

But God, who is rich in mercy, because of His great love with which He loved us, even when we were dead in trespasses, made us alive together with Christ (by grace you have been saved), and raised us up together, and made us sit together in the heavenly places in Christ Jesus. (Ephesians 2:4-6 NKJV)

When Jesus left this earth, He sat down at God's right hand. Sitting down signifies rest.

He didn't sit down because He was tired; He sat down because He was finished. The Bible says that as He is, so are we in this world (1 John 4:17). The above verse also says that when you were saved, you were raised up and made to sit together in the heavenly places in Christ Jesus.

In other words, you are at a place of rest. That's how you are like Christ. Your physical body and your emotions may be on this earth, but your spirit is one with Him in the heavenlies.

But he who is joined to the Lord is one spirit with Him.
(1 Corinthians 6:17 NKJV)

Where are you right now? You are seated at the right hand of the Father in Christ! God, by His grace, raised us up together and made us to sit together in the heavenly places in Christ.

Because as He is, so are we in this world.
(1 John 4:17 NKJV)

Christ is at rest and so should we be. Jesus is not filled with negative emotions. He's not worried. He's not anxious. He's not depressed. He's not sick. He's not suicidal. He's not sad. He's not complaining. He's not filled with sorrow. He's not filled with grief. He's not frustrated. He's not angry. He's not hateful. He's not impatient. He's not resentful or unforgiving.

He is at total rest. He's sitting down. And so are you!

So, you're not worried because He's not worried. You're not anxious, depressed, sick, suicidal, sad, complaining, sorrowful, filled with grief, frustrated, angry, hateful, impatient, resentful, or unforgiving because Jesus is not any of those things. As He is seated at the right hand of the Father, so are you in this world if you will just rest in the finished works of Christ.

You don't have to be free; you are already free!

NOW GO FEEL FREE!

TERRY TOLER

#1 AMAZON BEST SELLER

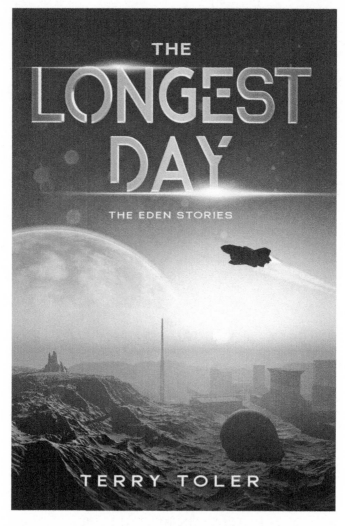

WINNER 2020 BEST BOOK AWARD FOR RELIGIOUS
FICTION

BEHOLDINGS PUBLISHING

Follow Terry at terrytoler.com.

Made in the USA
Monee, IL
10 June 2022

97790545R00121